TOP TRUMPS®

Indiana Jones

This book is officially licensed by Winning Moves UK Ltd,
owners of the Top Trumps registered trademark.

Benjamin Harper has asserted his right
to be identified as the author of this book.

First published in November 2008

British Library Cataloguing-in-Publication Data:
A catalogue record for this book is available from the British Library

ISBN 978 1 84425 684 6

Library of Congress catalog card no. 2008936573

Published by Haynes Publishing,
Sparkford, Yeovil, Somerset BA22 7JJ, UK
Tel: 01963 442030 Fax: 01963 440001
Int. tel: +44 1963 442030 Int. fax: +44 1963 440001
Email: sales@haynes.co.uk
Website: www.haynes.co.uk

Haynes North America, Inc.,
861 Lawrence Drive, Newbury Park, California 91320, USA

Designed by Lee Parsons

Printed and bound in Great Britain by J. H. Haynes & Co. Ltd, Sparkford

The Author

Benjamin Harper is an editor at DC Comics and author. Other *Indiana Jones* titles
he's written include *Indiana Jones and the Kingdom of the Crystal Skull Movie
Storybook* and *Race For Akator*. He currently lives in New York City.

TOP TRUMPS

INDIANA JONES

CONTENTS

ABOUT TOP TRUMPS

It's now more than 30 years since Britain's kids first caught the Top Trumps craze. The game remained hugely popular until the 1990s, when it slowly drifted into obscurity. Then, in 1999, UK games company Winning Moves discovered it, bought it, dusted it down, gave it a thorough makeover and introduced it to a whole new generation. And so the Top Trumps legend continues.

Nowadays, there are Top Trumps titles for just about everyone, with subjects about animals, cars, ships, aircraft and all the great films and TV shows. Top Trumps is now even more popular than before. In Britain, a pack of Top Trumps is bought every six seconds! And it's not just British children who love the game. Children in Australasia, the Far East, the Middle East, all over Europe and in North America can buy Top Trumps at their local shops.

Today you can even play the game on the internet, interactive DVD, your games console and even your mobile phone.

YOU'VE PLAYED THE GAME...

NOW READ THE BOOK!

Haynes Publishing and Top Trumps have teamed up to bring you this exciting new Top Trumps book, in which you will find even more pictures, details and statistics.

Top Trumps: Indiana Jones features 45 characters from the hugely successful *Indiana Jones* film series – from Indiana Jones, Marion Ravenwood and Short Round to Dr. René Belloq and Irina Spalko. Packed with fascinating facts, stunning photographs and all the vital statistics, this is the essential pocket guide.

Look out for other Top Trumps books from Haynes Publishing – even more facts, even more fun!

INDIANA JONES

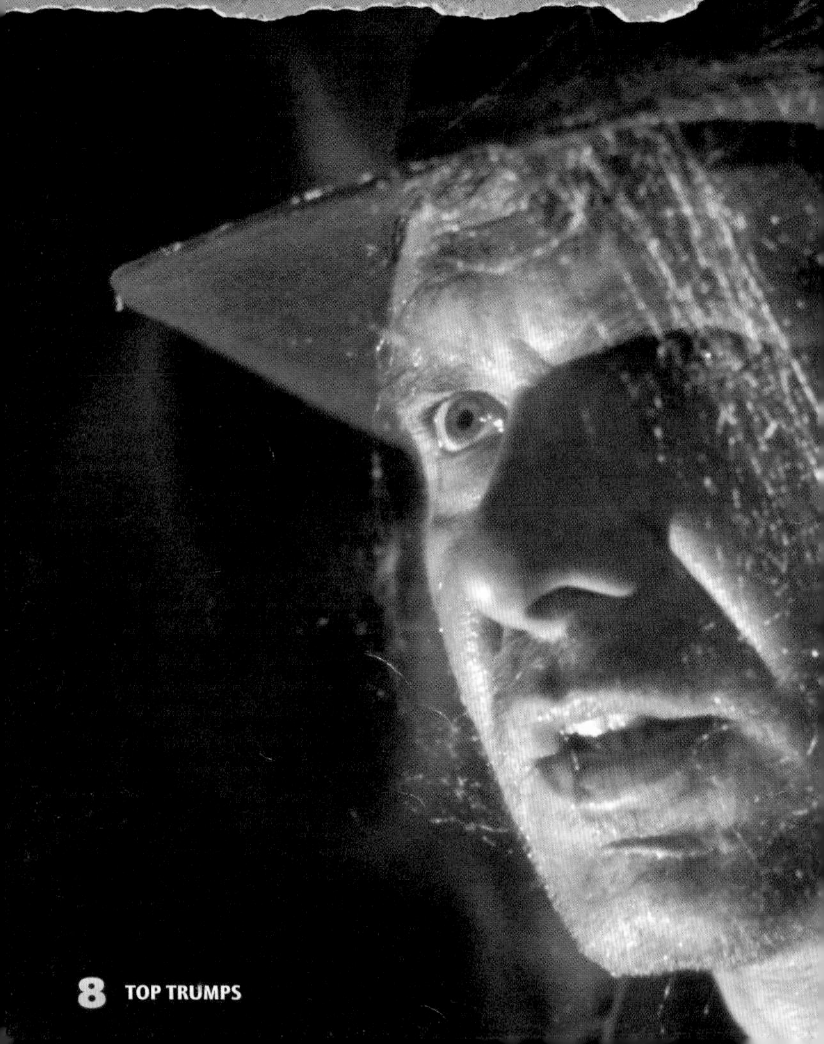

INDIANA JONES

Dr. Henry Walton Jones, Jr., or "Indiana" as he liked to be called, was born in 1899 in Princeton, New Jersey. He grew up to be a globe-travelling archaeologist, adventurer and explorer who was famous from Madagascar to Shanghai for his exceptional abilities. When he wasn't scouring the globe for treasure, he was a highly popular Professor of Archaeology at Marshall College in Connecticut. Although highly respected and sought-after as a professor, he was frequently absent from his classes when his services were required elsewhere.

Among Indiana's most famous adventures were his trip to Pankot Palace in India where he helped overthrow a Thuggee cult and recover sacred Sankara stones, his mission to Cairo to discover the resting place of the Ark of the Covenant before the Nazis could acquire it, and his rescue mission to Venice where he sought to locate his kidnapped father before the two of them went on a quest to find the Holy Grail. Jones also raced against the KGB during the Cold War in an attempt to return a magical crystal skull to the lost city of Akator before the Russians could use its legendary powers to control the world.

STATISTICS

APPEARANCES:	*Indiana Jones and the Raiders of the Lost Ark, Indiana Jones and the Temple of Doom, Indiana Jones and the Last Crusade, Indiana Jones and the Kingdom of the Crystal Skull*
STRENGTH LEVEL:	**9**
INTELLIGENCE LEVEL:	**10**
SKILLS:	**10** Archaeology, Hand-to-hand combat, Espionage, Weaponry
EQUIPMENT:	**8** Whip, Pistol
SECONDARY SKILLS:	**10** Vehicle Operation, Navigation
ALLEGIANCE:	Archaeology
ENEMIES:	Chattar Lal, Mola Ram, Zalim Singh, Dr. René Belloq, Herman Dietrich, Elsa Schneider, Walter Donovan, Irina Spalko, Antonin Dovchenko, Snakes
ALLIES:	Short Round, Willie Scott, Marion Ravenwood, Dr. Marcus Brody, Sallah Mohammed Faisel el-Kahir, Simon Katanga, Henry Jones, Sr., Mutt Williams, Dr. Harold Oxley, Dean Charles Stanforth
LINE:	**"Why did it have to be snakes?"**

MARION RAVENWOOD

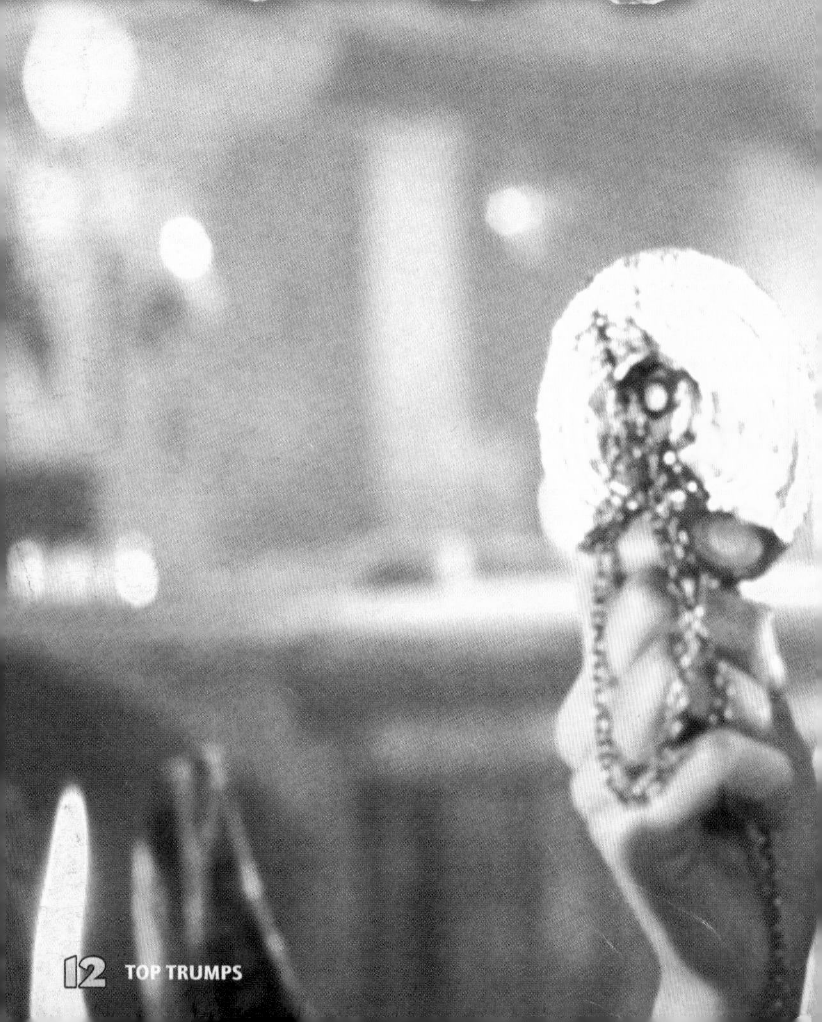

MARION RAVENWOOD

The daughter of one of Indiana Jones' professors at the University of Chicago, Marion Ravenwood travelled the world with her father, Abner, as he searched for treasure and for clues that would lead him to the lost Ark of the Covenant. At one point Marion had been romantically involved with Indiana, but he left her, and she continued travelling with her father. Their journeys brought them to Nepal, where Marion was stranded after Abner died in an avalanche. She made a meager living by running the Raven Tavern until one evening when Indiana came back, searching for the headpiece to the Staff of Ra. She refused to give it to him, but Nazi agents who came into her bar and threatened to kill her made her change her mind. She followed Jones to Cairo and helped him recover the Ark. Afterwards, she returned to the United States with him, but he abandoned her again a week before they were to be married.

She was reunited with Jones again in 1957 deep in the rain forest of Peru after she sent her son Mutt Williams to find him. She knew Jones would be the only person smart enough to rescue her and her friend Harold Oxley from the clutches of the KGB. After they met again, she revealed to Indiana that Mutt was in actuality Henry Jones III, his son. Their old sparks were reignited and the two were finally married.

STATISTICS

APPEARANCES:	*Indiana Jones and the Raiders of the Lost Ark, Indiana Jones and the Kingdom of the Crystal Skull*
STRENGTH LEVEL:	**7**
INTELLIGENCE LEVEL:	**10**
SKILLS:	**10** Hand-to-hand combat, Weaponry
EQUIPMENT:	**7** Pistol, Frying pan
SECONDARY SKILLS:	**9** Tactical, Vehicle operation
ALLEGIANCE:	Indiana Jones
ENEMIES:	Dr. René Belloq, Herman Dietrich, Arnold Ernst Toht, Irina Spalko, Antonin Dovchenko
ALLIES:	Indiana Jones, Sallah Mohammed Faisel el-Kahir, Mutt Williams, Harold Oxley
LINE:	**"See you tomorrow, Indiana Jones."**

DR. MARCUS BRODY

DR. MARCUS BRODY

Dr. Marcus Brody was curator of the National Museum in 1936 when he and Indiana Jones were approached by U.S. government agents who hoped the two of them would be able to decipher a Nazi communiqué that had been intercepted by government operatives overseas. Brody and Jones impressed the agents with their knowledge of Tanis and the Ark of the Covenant, and Brody had the pleasure of telling Indiana that the U.S. government had hired him to recover the Ark of the Covenant before the Nazis could get it.

In 1938, Brody accompanied Indiana Jones to Venice, Italy, after learning that Jones' father, Henry Jones, Sr., had disappeared after being hired to locate the Holy Grail. While Jones went in search of his father, Brody travelled to Iskenderun to hire Sallah Mohammed Faisel el-Kahir to help retrieve the Holy Grail. Brody was kidnapped by the Nazis and eventually rescued by Sallah, Indiana and Henry Jones, Sr. He ran into the Nazis one final time as they reached the final resting place of the Holy Grail, where the Nazis were defeated and the Grail left in its rightful place.

STATISTICS

APPEARANCES:	*Indiana Jones and the Raiders of the Lost Ark, Indiana Jones and the Last Crusade*
STRENGTH LEVEL:	**5**
INTELLIGENCE LEVEL:	**10**
SKILLS:	**10** Historical knowledge
EQUIPMENT:	None
SECONDARY SKILLS:	**9** Wit
ALLEGIANCE:	Indiana Jones
ENEMIES:	Walter Donovan, Colonel Ernst Vogel
ALLIES:	Henry Jones, Sr., Indiana Jones, Sallah Mohammed Faisel el-Kadir
LINE:	**"The pen is mightier than the sword!"**

DR. RENÉ BELLOQ

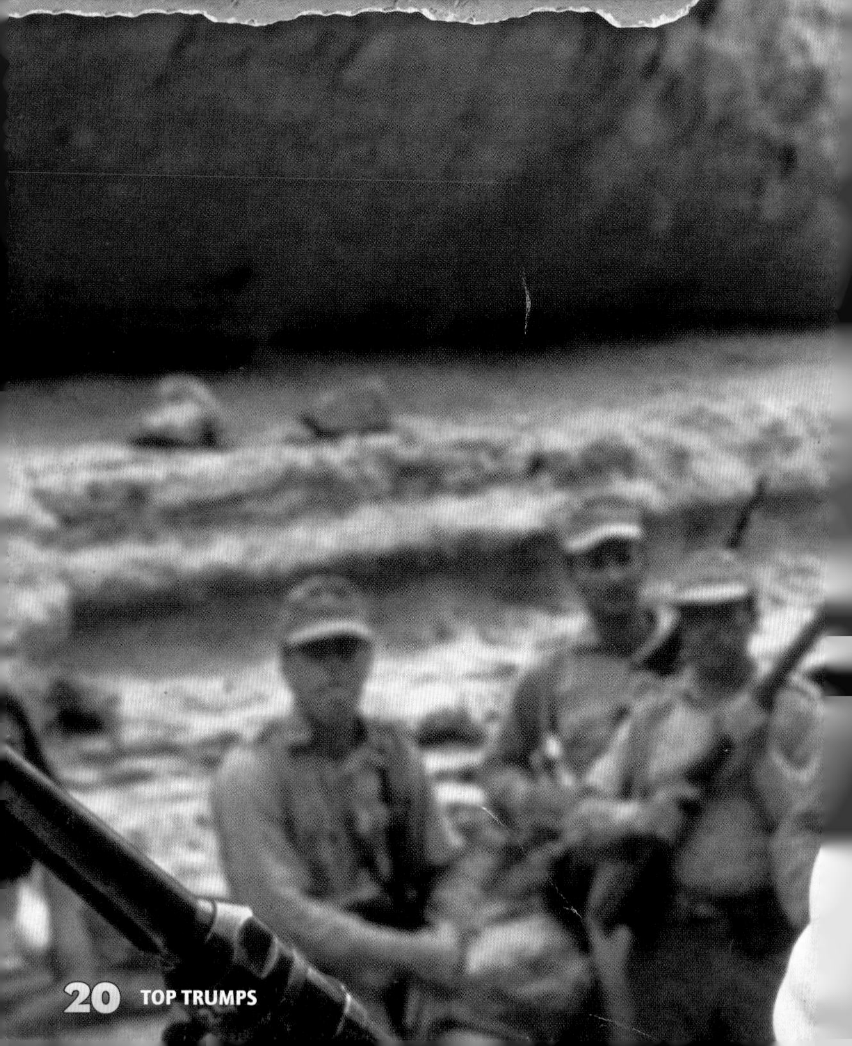

DR. RENÉ BELLOQ

One of Indiana Jones' primary archaeological nemeses, Dr. René Belloq met Jones outside a Chachapoyan Temple with a tribe of Hovitos and took a golden idol from Jones before directing the Hovitos warriors to chase and kill him.

Indiana ran into Belloq again when searching for the Ark of the Covenant in Tanis. Belloq had been hired by the Nazis to locate the Ark. After discovering he had been digging in the wrong place, Belloq took the Ark from Jones. Belloq and the Nazis carried the Ark to a secret Nazi island base, where Belloq performed an ancient ritual to test its authenticity. As he performed the ritual, strange spirits escaped the Ark, and then killed Belloq and all of his Nazi onlookers. Only Indiana Jones and Marion Ravenwood, who were being held prisoner, survived – Indiana told Marion not to look at the spirits of the Ark under any circumstances. After Belloq and the Nazis were dead, the Ark sealed itself and fell silent.

STATISTICS

APPEARANCE:	*Indiana Jones and the Raiders of the Lost Ark*
STRENGTH LEVEL:	6
INTELLIGENCE LEVEL:	10
SKILLS:	10 Archaeology
EQUIPMENT:	7 Machine gun
SECONDARY SKILLS:	8 Multiple languages, Diplomacy
ALLEGIANCE:	Nazis
ENEMIES:	Indiana Jones, Marion Ravenwood
ALLIES:	Herman Dietrich, Arnold Ernst Toht, Hovitos
LINE:	**"Dr. Jones. Again we see there is nothing you can possess which I cannot take away."**

SALLAH MOHAMMED FAISEL EL-KAHIR

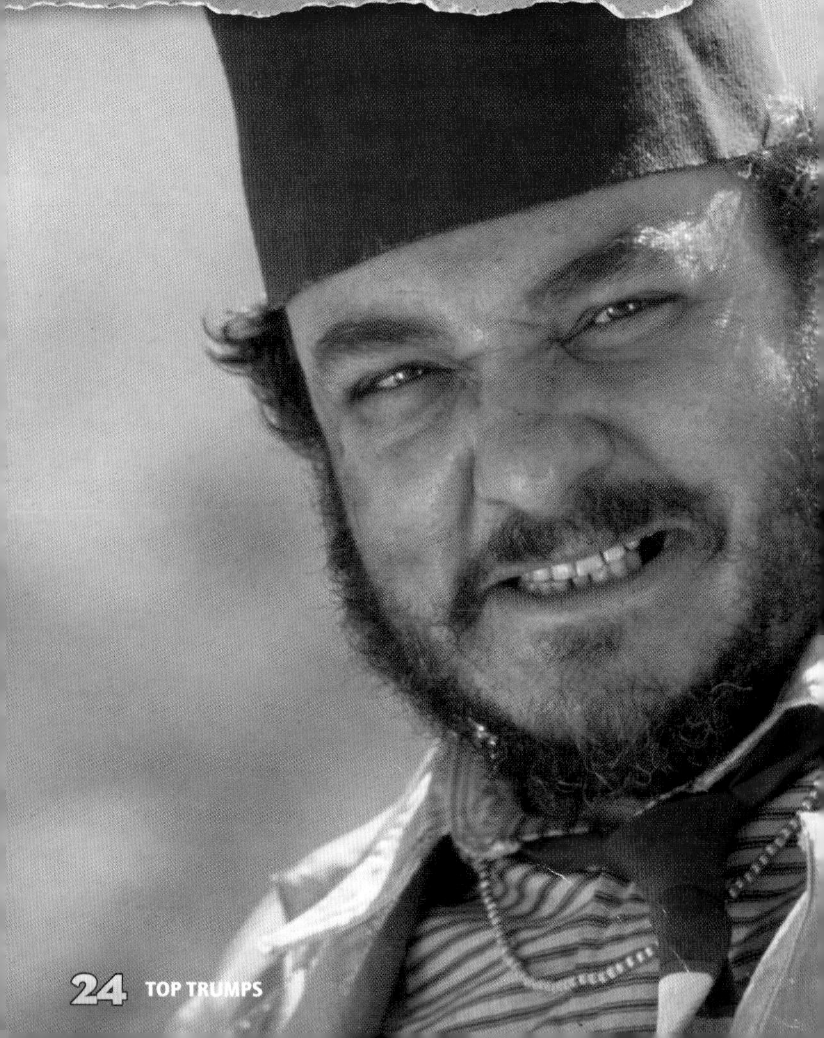

Longtime friend of Indiana Jones, Sallah was, according to Dr. Jones, the "best digger in Egypt." Sallah lived in Cairo with his wife Fayah and their children. He helped Indy and Marion when they arrived in Egypt on their quest for the Ark of the Covenant, immediately bringing the archaeologist up to date on the Nazis' progress in their search for Tanis and the Well of Souls. Sallah also helped Jones find a translator for the ancient language on the headpiece of the Staff of Ra, which enabled Dr. Jones to find the Well of Souls before the Nazis. After discovering the location of the Ark, Jones enlisted Sallah to round up workers. Together, they retrieved the Ark. After many struggles, Indiana finally gained possession of the Ark and Sallah found Jones and Marion safe passage aboard Simon Katanga's ship.

Sallah helped Dr. Jones on many other adventures, including Jones' search for the Holy Grail. Sallah took Dr. Jones and his father through the desert in search of Marcus Brody, who had been captured by Nazis, and ultimately helped Indiana and his father defeat the Nazis, allowing the grail to stay in its intended resting place.

STATISTICS

APPEARANCES:	*Indiana Jones and the Raiders of the Lost Ark, Indiana Jones and the Last Crusade*
STRENGTH LEVEL:	**9**
INTELLIGENCE LEVEL:	**8**
SKILLS:	**9** Archaeological excavation, Guide
EQUIPMENT:	**9** Pickaxe, Shovel
SECONDARY SKILLS:	**9** Hospitality, Loyalty
ALLEGIANCE:	Indiana Jones
ENEMIES:	Nazis
ALLIES:	Indiana Jones, Marcus Brody, Marion Ravenwood, Dr. Henry Jones, Sr.
LINE:	**"Bad dates."**

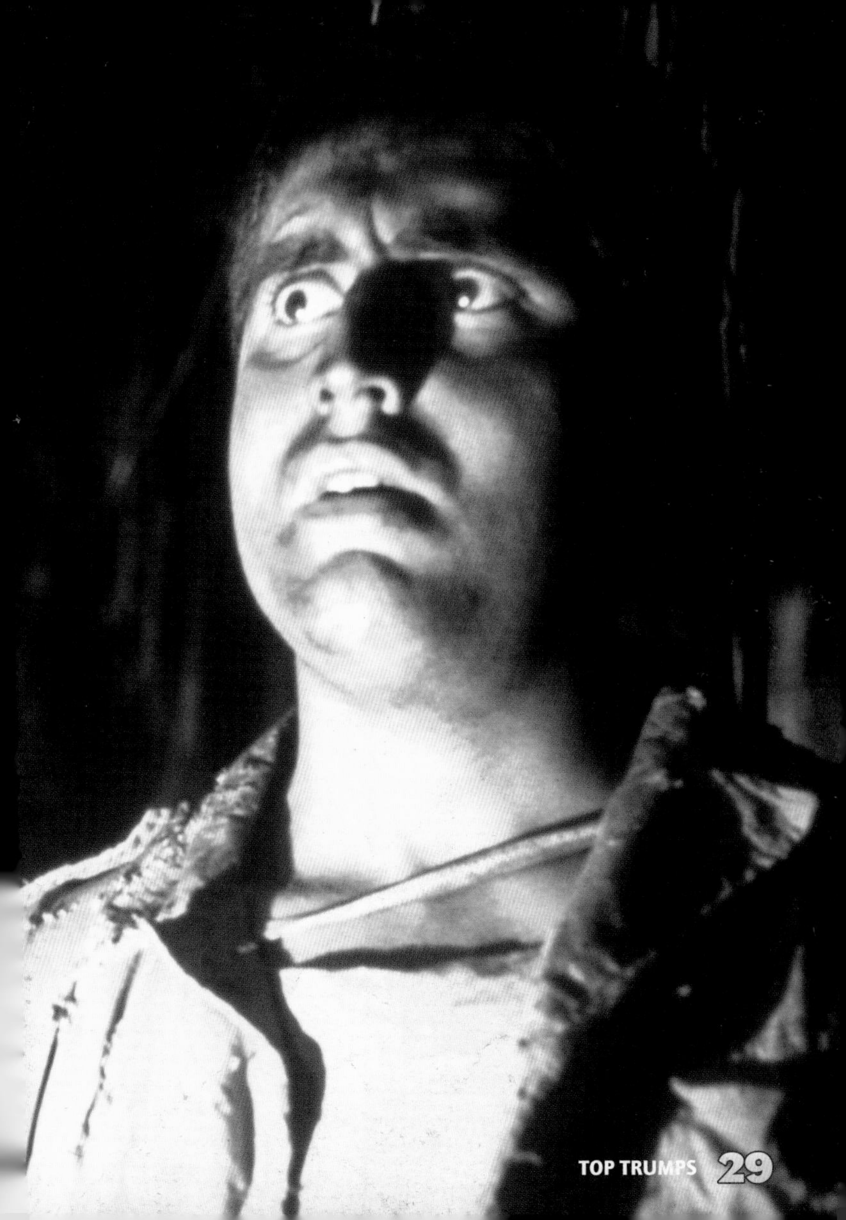

SATIPO

This con man did most of his misdeeds from an Amazonian outpost called Machete Junction. Satipo had a fragment of a map that allegedly lead to the Chachapoyan temple and to treasure beyond anyone's imagination. Indiana Jones, who held another portion of the map, hired Satipo to help him find the temple despite the guide's bad reputation, in order to combine the map fragments and find the temple. When Jones and his party found the entrance, Satipo accompanied him inside.

Satipo appeared to be a proper assistant until, after the pair set off several traps within the temple, he talked Dr. Jones into throwing him a rare golden idol. Taking the idol, he left Jones dangling over the edge of a pit. No longer cautious, Satipo fell prey to one of the temple's traps, and Jones got the idol after all.

STATISTICS

APPEARANCE:	*Indiana Jones and the Raiders of the Lost Ark*
STRENGTH LEVEL:	**6**
INTELLIGENCE LEVEL:	**6**
SKILLS:	**6** Jungle guide
EQUIPMENT:	**7** Machete, Canteen, Hiking equipment
SECONDARY SKILLS:	**6** Conning, Thievery
ALLEGIANCE:	Money
ENEMIES:	Explorers, Hovitos
ALLIES:	Barranca – his partner in crime
LINE:	**"Adios, señor."**

COLONEL HERMAN DIETRICH

COLONEL HERMAN DIETRICH

Already acquainted with the French archaeologist, Colonel Herman Dietrich was assigned the very important task of working with Dr. René Belloq to retrieve the coveted Ark of the Covenant for Der Führer, Adolf Hitler. When he and Belloq arrived in Cairo, the dig for the Ark was already under way. The Colonel did not know the Nazis were digging in the wrong place until Belloq discovered an unauthorized dig in the distance from their site. The Nazis rushed to the site and took the Ark from Dr. Jones. Colonel Dietrich then hurled Marion Ravenwood into the deep chamber with Dr. Jones and sealed them both in. Later, after Indy escaped, he chased Dietrich and Belloq and regained possession of the Ark, only to have it snatched away again aboard the *Bantu Wind*.

Dietrich watched on as Dr. Belloq performed an ancient ritual over the Ark of the Covenant on a secret island base. He hadn't been prepared for such devastating results, and as spirits released from the Ark flew around him and his troops, he perished.

STATISTICS

APPEARANCE:	*Indiana Jones and the Raiders of the Lost Ark*
STRENGTH LEVEL:	7
INTELLIGENCE LEVEL:	7
SKILLS:	**8** Military Leadership
EQUIPMENT:	None
SECONDARY SKILLS:	**8** Intimidation
ALLEGIANCE:	Nazis
ENEMIES:	Indiana Jones, Marion Ravenwood, Simon Katanga
ALLIES:	Major Ernst Toht, Dr. René Belloq, Adolf Hitler
LINE:	**"Only our mission for the Führer matters."**

MAJOR ARNOLD ERNST TOHT

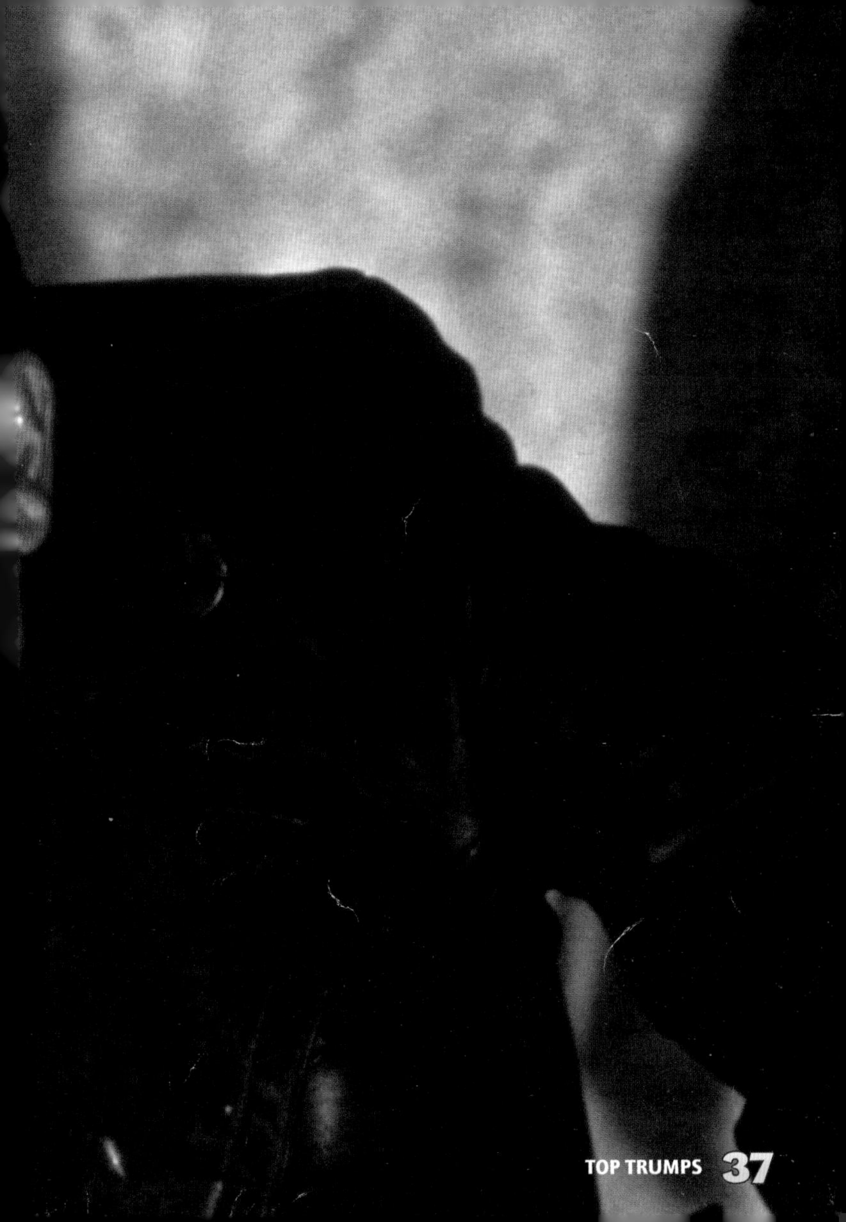

MAJOR ARNOLD ERNST TOHT

Arnold Ernst Toht was a Nazi agent who followed Indiana Jones to Marion Ravenwood's saloon in Nepal. Like Jones, Toht was on a quest for the headpiece to the Staff of Ra. After Jones left Marion's bar, Toht threatened her for the piece, but before she could talk, Indiana came in and rescued her. Toht and his thugs fought Marion and Indiana for the piece, but he came up empty-handed. He saw the piece on the floor near an out-of-control fire, and when he attempted to grab it, he seared his hand. He ran out of the bar in pain and thrust his hand into the snow.

Toht was on hand during the Nazi excavation in Cairo, where the Nazis ultimately secured the Ark, but only after Indiana Jones had discovered its location. On a secret island base, Toht observed as Dr. René Belloq performed an ancient ritual over the Ark in order to prove its authenticity. Toht, incredulous at the beginning, soon felt the Ark's power, and perished on the island.

STATISTICS

APPEARANCE:	*Indiana Jones and the Raiders of the Lost Ark*
STRENGTH LEVEL:	6
INTELLIGENCE LEVEL:	8
SKILLS:	9 Intimidation
EQUIPMENT:	6 Pistol
SECONDARY SKILLS:	8 Espionage
ALLEGIANCE:	Nazis
ENEMIES:	Indiana Jones
ALLIES:	Nazis, Dr. René Belloq
LINE:	**"Fraulein Ravenwood, let me show you what I am used to."**

BARRANCA

BARRANCA

Barranca was part of a duo of thugs based in Machete Junction, a landing in the South American jungle. Along with his partner, Satipo, Barranca lured gullible explorers into the jungle with promises of finding great treasure. If any explorer ever actually found anything, Barranca planned to steal the treasure and do away with the hapless explorer deep in the jungle.

Barranca accompanied Indiana Jones on his quest for the Chachapoyan temple but attempted to steal the map from him, pulling a gun on the explorer. Jones whipped the gun out of Barranca's hand, sending the thief fleeing into the jungle. Jones and Satipo continued into the temple's depths.

When Dr. Jones finally escaped the temple's many dangers, he found Barranca killed at the hands of the Hovitos tribe and his arch-rival, Dr. René Belloq.

STATISTICS

APPEARANCE:	*Indiana Jones and the Raiders of the Lost Ark*
STRENGTH LEVEL:	**6**
INTELLIGENCE LEVEL:	**7**
SKILLS:	**6** Jungle Guide
EQUIPMENT:	**6** Gun
SECONDARY SKILLS:	**6** Thievery
ALLEGIANCE:	Money
ENEMIES:	Explorers, Hovitos, Dr. René Belloq
ALLIES:	Satipo, his partner in crime
LINE:	**"If they knew we were here, they would have killed us already."**

MAJOR GOBLER

Major Gobler was personal assistant to Colonel Dietrich during the Nazis' dig for the Ark of the Covenant in Tanis. Like Dietrich, he had little interest in the Ark other than retrieving it for Hitler. After the Nazis had taken the Ark from Jones and considered him sealed under the earth forever, they were surprised when a Flying Wing airplane exploded. They realized that Jones had escaped, so Gobler had the Ark placed on a truck and taken away immediately under Colonel Dietrich's orders. Not to be stopped, Jones chased the Nazi convoy. After a long and harrowing fight, Gobler's car sped out of control and flew over a cliff. Jones managed to evade the Nazis and drive the truck carrying the Ark to safety – at least temporarily.

STATISTICS

APPEARANCE:	*Indiana Jones and the Raiders of the Lost Ark*
STRENGTH LEVEL:	**7**
INTELLIGENCE LEVEL:	6
SKILLS:	**6** Servitude
EQUIPMENT:	**4** Car
SECONDARY SKILLS:	**8** Loyalty
ALLEGIANCE:	Nazis
ENEMIES:	Indiana Jones
ALLIES:	Arnold Ernst Toht, Herman Dietrich, Adolf Hitler
LINE:	**"Jawohl!"**

SIMON KATANGA

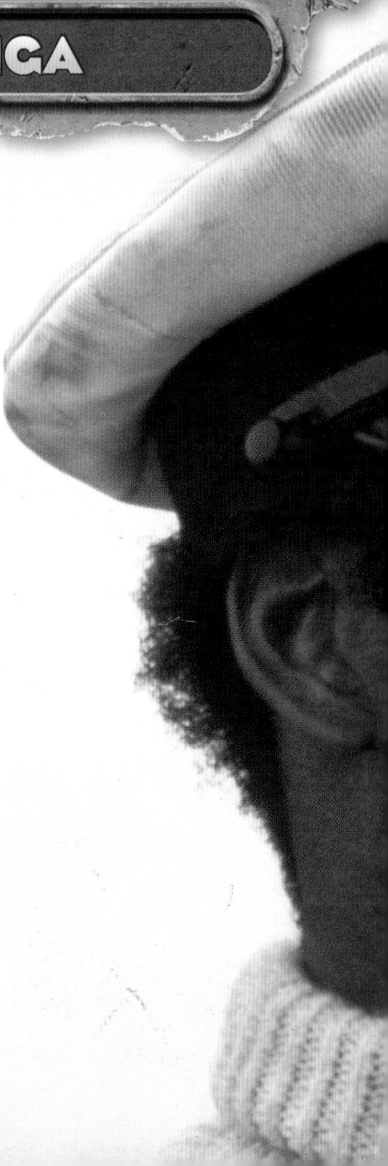

SIMON KATANGA

After Indiana Jones managed to retrieve the Ark of the Covenant from the Nazis, he needed safe and discreet passage from Cairo. His friend Sallah arranged for that passage, and Indiana, along with Marion and the Ark, boarded the *Bantu Wind* – a ship captained by Simon Katanga.

Katanga promised Sallah that his friends would be treated well. However, when Nazis caught up with Katanga at sea, he played the role of modern-day pirate. After Nazis boarded and searched his ship, taking back the Ark, Katanga lied to the soldiers, telling them he had killed Indiana Jones. He asked the Nazis to leave Marion on his ship, but they took her and the Ark. When Katanga asked his crew to find Indiana Jones, one of them pointed – Jones had jumped ship and was on the Nazi submarine.

STATISTICS

APPEARANCE:	*Indiana Jones and the Raiders of the Lost Ark*
STRENGTH LEVEL:	**8**
INTELLIGENCE LEVEL:	**8**
SKILLS:	**9** Commanding the *Bantu Wind*
EQUIPMENT:	**8** The *Bantu Wind*
SECONDARY SKILLS:	None
ALLEGIANCE:	Indiana Jones
ENEMIES:	Nazis
ALLIES:	Sallah, Indiana Jones, Marion Ravenwood
LINE:	**"Mr. Jones – I've heard a lot about you, sir. Your appearance is exactly as I had imagined!"**

WILLIE SCOTT

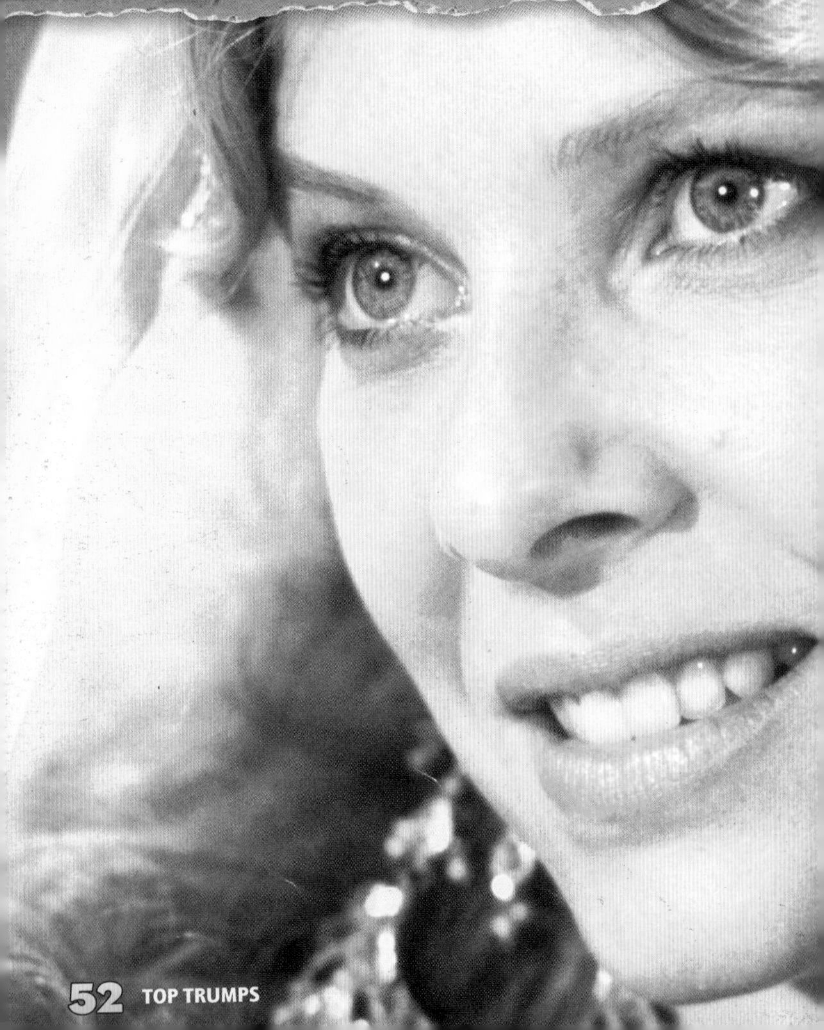

WILLIE SCOTT

Wilhelmina Scott, "Willie" for short, was a professional singer originally from Missouri who was performing in Club Obi Wan the night Indiana Jones entered into dangerous negotiations with its owner, Lao Che. A fight ensued and Scott, Jones and his sidekick Short Round escaped Shanghai on a plane, only to find, in mid-flight, that its pilots had emptied the fuel tanks and parachuted out. They evacuated in a liferaft, landing in India. There, Scott was an unwilling companion as Jones went to Pankot Palace to retrieve sacred stones. Scott was captured by the frightful Thuggee cult at Pankot and almost lowered into molten lava as a human sacrifice. After Short Round had rescued the adventurer, Jones rescued her in the nick of time and they escaped the palace. After Jones had outsmarted Mola Ram, head of the Thuggees, the rest of the cult was driven off by Captain Blumburtt and his troops. Scott accompanied Jones as he returned the sacred Sankara stone to its rightful place in an Indian village.

STATISTICS

APPEARANCE:	*Indiana Jones and the Temple of Doom*
STRENGTH LEVEL:	5
INTELLIGENCE LEVEL:	7
SKILLS:	**7** Singing, Dancing
EQUIPMENT:	None
SECONDARY SKILLS:	**8** Screaming, Whining
ALLEGIANCE:	Indiana Jones
ENEMIES:	Mola Ram, Thuggees
ALLIES:	Indiana Jones, Short Round
LINE:	**"I always thought archaeologists were funny little men searching for their mommies."**

SHORT ROUND

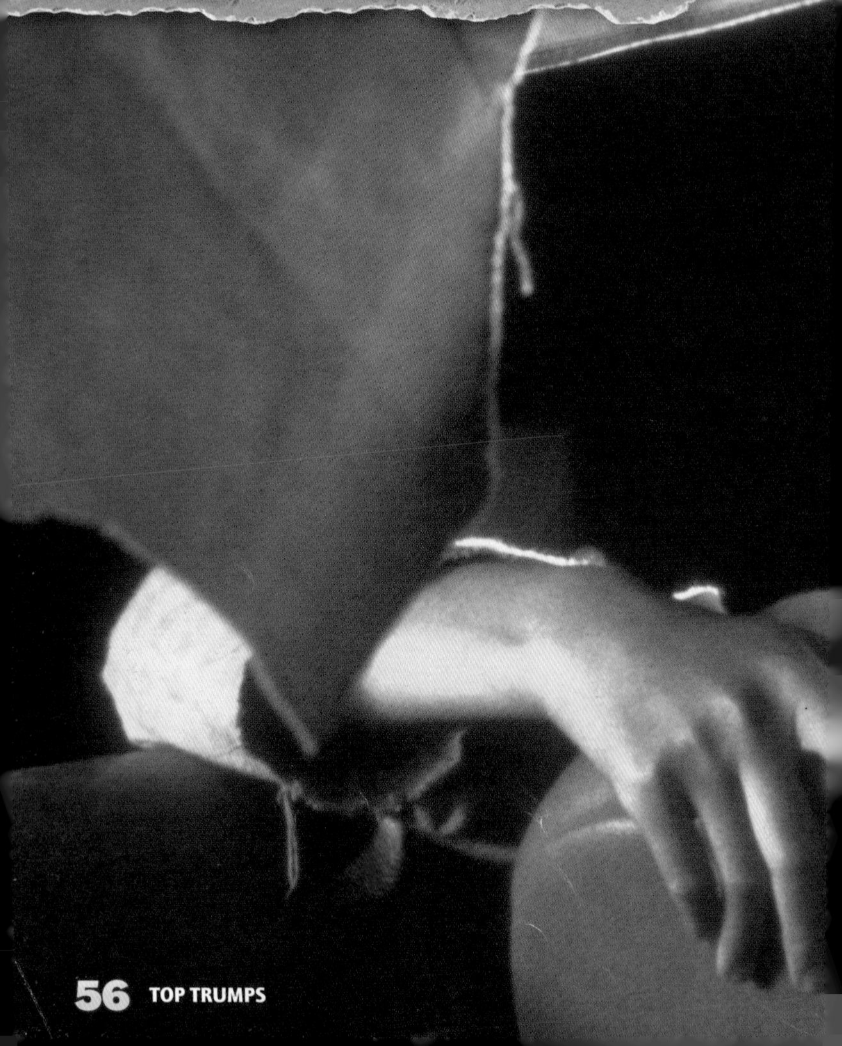

SHORT ROUND

Born Wan Li, Short Round was orphaned when his parents were killed in the bombing of Shanghai. He then grew up in the alleys of that exotic city, earning his nickname, "Short Round," by picking pockets. He met Dr. Jones after attempting to pick the archaeologist's pocket, and the two became good friends.

Short Round accompanied Dr. Jones and Willie on their adventure to Pankot Palace after driving them from the Club Obi Wan in a gun-shooting, high-speed chase. He saved Indiana from the brainwashing Thuggee cult by shocking him back to consciousness with a torch, and then by waking Maharajah Zalim Singh from his brainwashing – Singh had been using a voodoo doll to keep Jones in crippling pain. Short Round also helped Indy outsmart the Thuggees on a perilous bridge, translating his words in Chinese to English.

STATISTICS

APPEARANCE:	*Indiana Jones and the Temple of Doom*
STRENGTH LEVEL:	**6**
INTELLIGENCE LEVEL:	**8**
SKILLS:	**8** Bravery, Devotion
EQUIPMENT:	**9** Torch
SECONDARY SKILLS:	**8** Vehicle operation, Combat
ALLEGIANCE:	Indiana Jones
ENEMIES:	Mola Ram, Zalim Singh
ALLIES:	Indiana Jones, Willie Scott
LINE:	**"Very funny!"**

LAO CHE

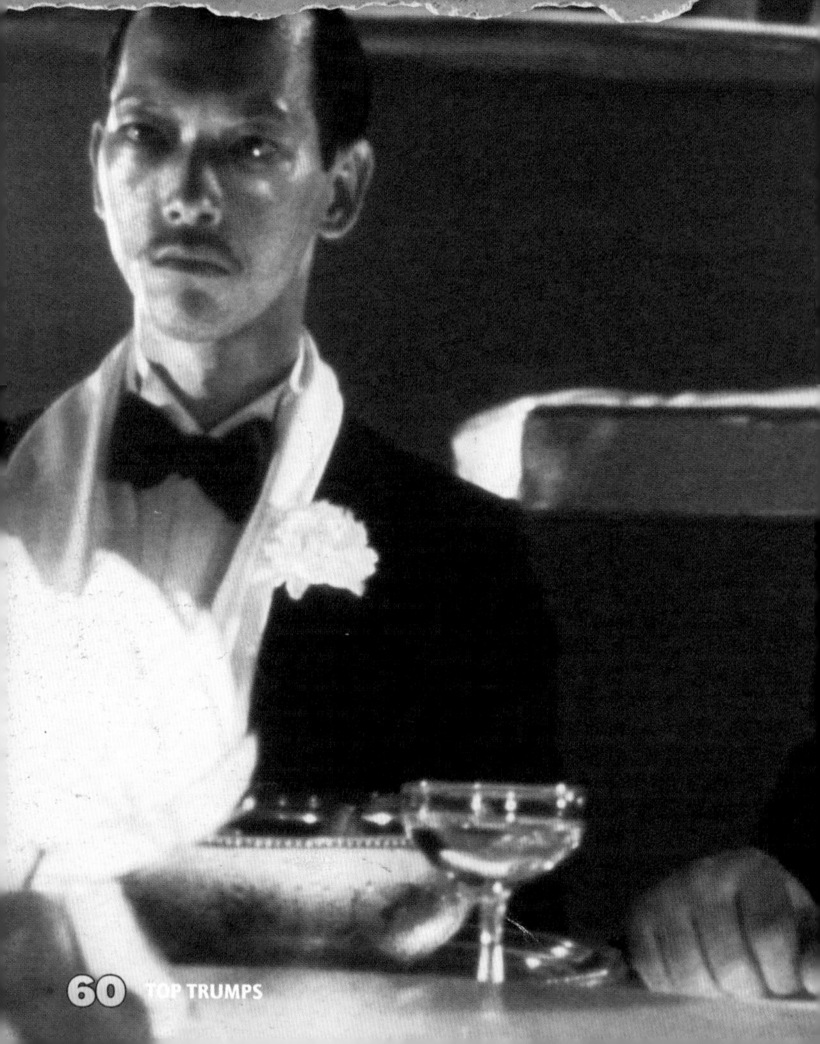

Lao Che went from being a petty Shanghai thief to one of the city's top crime lords, as well as owner of Club Obi Wan, the nightclub in which Willie Scott sang. Che had hired Indiana Jones to recover the remains of Nurhachi, the first emperor of the Manchu dynasty, in exchange for the Eye of the Peacock diamond. Che initially wanted to double-cross Jones, sending one of his sons to steal the ashes, but the attempt failed. Jones then met Che in Club Obi Wan, where, when facing another double-cross, Jones grabbed and threatened Che's girlfriend, Willie. Che gave Jones the diamond, but asked for it back in exchange for an antidote to the poison he had placed in Jones' celebratory cocktail. A violent skirmish ensued, leaving Che angered over the death of his son, and Jones on the run with the antidote and Willie in tow.

STATISTICS

APPEARANCE:	*Indiana Jones and the Temple of Doom*
STRENGTH LEVEL:	**6**
INTELLIGENCE LEVEL:	**9**
SKILLS:	**9** Business, Crime
EQUIPMENT:	None
SECONDARY SKILLS:	**9** Double-crossing
ALLEGIANCE:	Crime
ENEMIES:	Indiana Jones
ALLIES:	Chen, Kao Kan
LINE:	**"The poison works fast, Dr. Jones."**

WU HAN

WU HAN

Wu Han was a friend of Indiana Jones and followed him on many adventures, including the search for a living dinosaur. Wu Han had at one time been indentured to Lao Che when Che stole his family's ashes and offered proper burial only if Wu Han would be his servant. After hearing this story, Indiana Jones stole the ashes back, releasing Wu Han from Lao Che's grasp.

Later, when Jones was face to face with crime lord Lao Che in Club Obi Wan, he knew the crime lord would try to double-cross him. Wu Han, posing as a waiter, stood by and watched. When trouble started, Wu Han, at Jones' side, very discreetly revealed a gun under his tray, hoping to end the disagreement. Things went awry, and Lao Che's son shot Wu Han. Indiana Jones held Wu Han as he died.

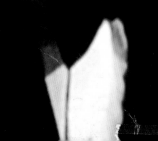

STATISTICS

APPEARANCE:	*Indiana Jones and the Temple of Doom*
STRENGTH LEVEL:	**6**
INTELLIGENCE LEVEL:	**7**
SKILLS:	**7** Disguise
EQUIPMENT:	**7** Pistol
SECONDARY SKILLS:	**9** Loyalty
ALLEGIANCE:	Indiana Jones
ENEMIES:	Lao Che, Chen, Kao Kan
ALLIES:	Indiana Jones
LINE:	**"I followed you on many adventures but into the great unknown mystery, I go first, Indy!"**

CHATTAR LAL

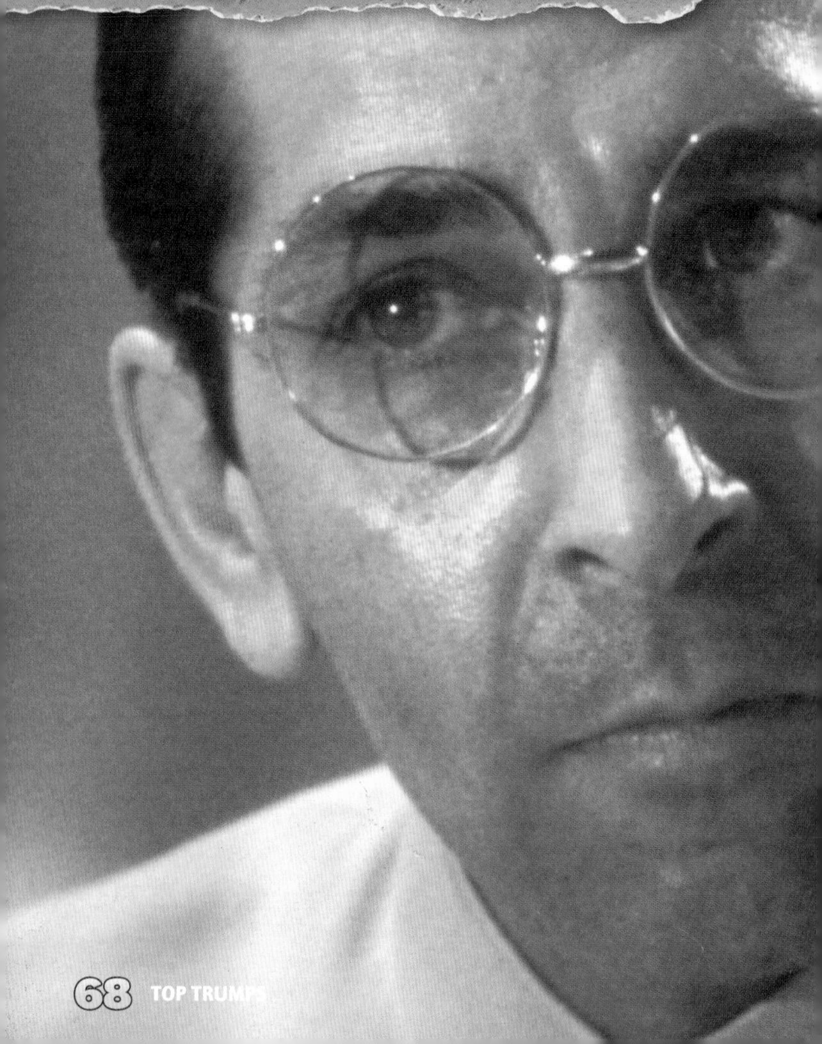

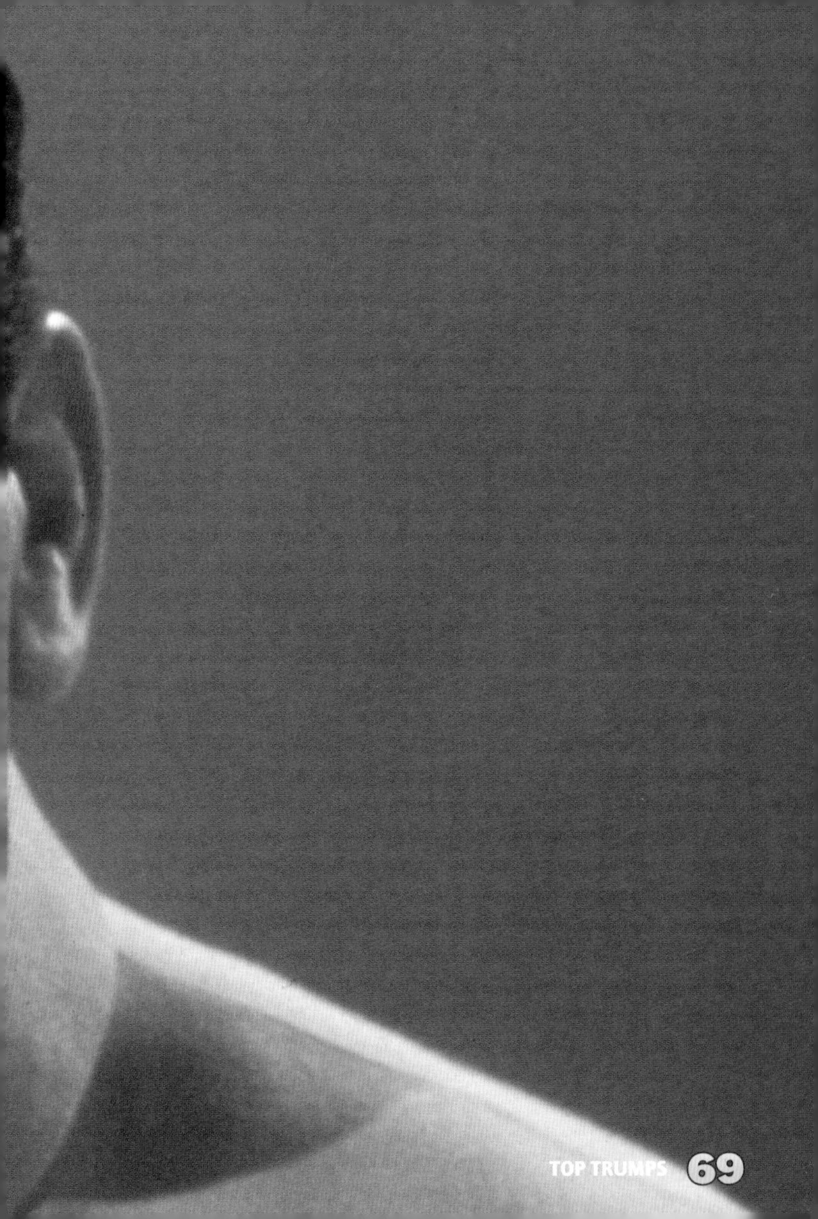

CHATTAR LAL

A well-mannered, soft-spoken and dapper gentleman, Chattar Lal was Prime Minster to the Pankot Province and chief advisor to Maharajah Zalim Singh. He received an education at Oxford University and was very well versed in Western culture. When Indiana Jones, Willie Scott and Short Round arrived at Pankot Palace, Chattar Lal greeted them graciously and welcomed them to stay.

After Jones asked about the Thuggee cult at dinner, Chattar Lal assured him that the death cult of Kali Ma had been eradicated, and then admonished Dr. Jones for being rude. However, Lal was a willing acolyte in the death cult, using his evil knowledge to create potions that brainwashed the young Maharajah into doing the cult's bidding. Lal and Jones fought in hand-to-hand combat in the temple deep beneath the palace, Jones defeating and wounding Lal. The evildoer apparently survived the battle, though he could do nothing to stop Jones from escaping.

STATISTICS

APPEARANCE:	*Indiana Jones and the Temple of Doom*
STRENGTH LEVEL:	6
INTELLIGENCE LEVEL:	9
SKILLS:	8 Diplomacy
EQUIPMENT:	5 Dagger
SECONDARY SKILLS:	8 Thuggee black magic arts
ALLEGIANCE:	Kali Ma
ENEMIES:	Indiana Jones, Willie Scott, Short Round
ALLIES:	Zalim Singh, Mola Ram
LINE:	**"Dr. Jones, you know perfectly well the Thuggee cult has been dead for nearly a century."**

MONKEY MAN

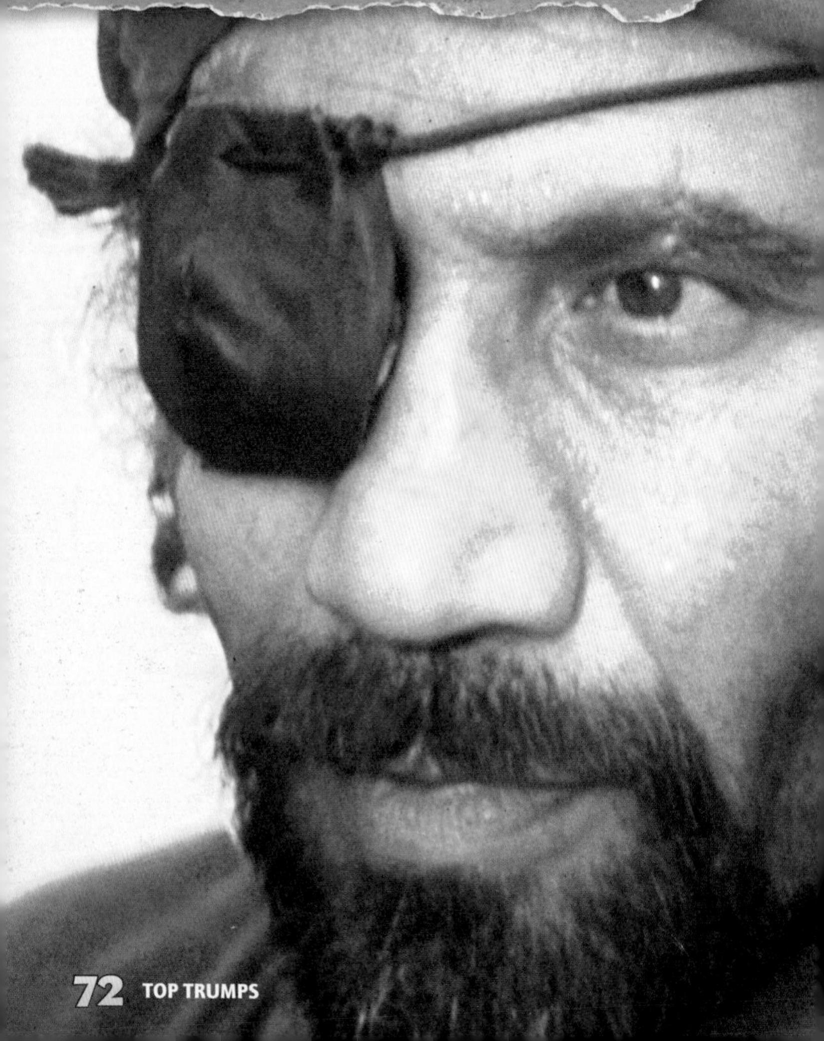

MONKEY MAN

The mysterious Monkey Man wore a patch over his right eye and rode a motorcycle. He was a Nazi operative and trailed Indiana Jones and Marion Ravenwood through the streets of Cairo, enlisting his pet monkey's help. The monkey took a liking to Marion, making it easy for the Monkey Man and his Nazi employers to find her. When Marion was on the run from Nazis and thugs in a Cairo market, she hid in a wicker basket only to be betrayed by the monkey, who climbed on top of the basket and shrieked until soldiers took the basket away.

After Marion's apparent death in the market chase, Sallah took Indiana to the house of an Imam in hopes that the learned scholar could translate the markings on the headpiece for the Staff of Ra. Monkey Man snuck into the old man's house and poisoned a bowl of dates, hoping to end Indiana Jones' search for the Ark. His plan backfired, however, when his pet monkey ate one of the tainted dates, alerting Sallah and Jones to the poison.

STATISTICS

APPEARANCE:	*Indiana Jones and the Raiders of the Lost Ark*
STRENGTH LEVEL:	**7**
INTELLIGENCE LEVEL:	**7**
SKILLS:	**8** Espionage
EQUIPMENT:	**6** Pet monkey
SECONDARY SKILLS:	**7** Stealth
ALLEGIANCE:	Nazis
ENEMIES:	Indiana Jones, Marion Ravenwood
ALLIES:	His pet monkey
LINE:	**"Sieg, Heil!"**

MAHARAJAH ZALIM SINGH

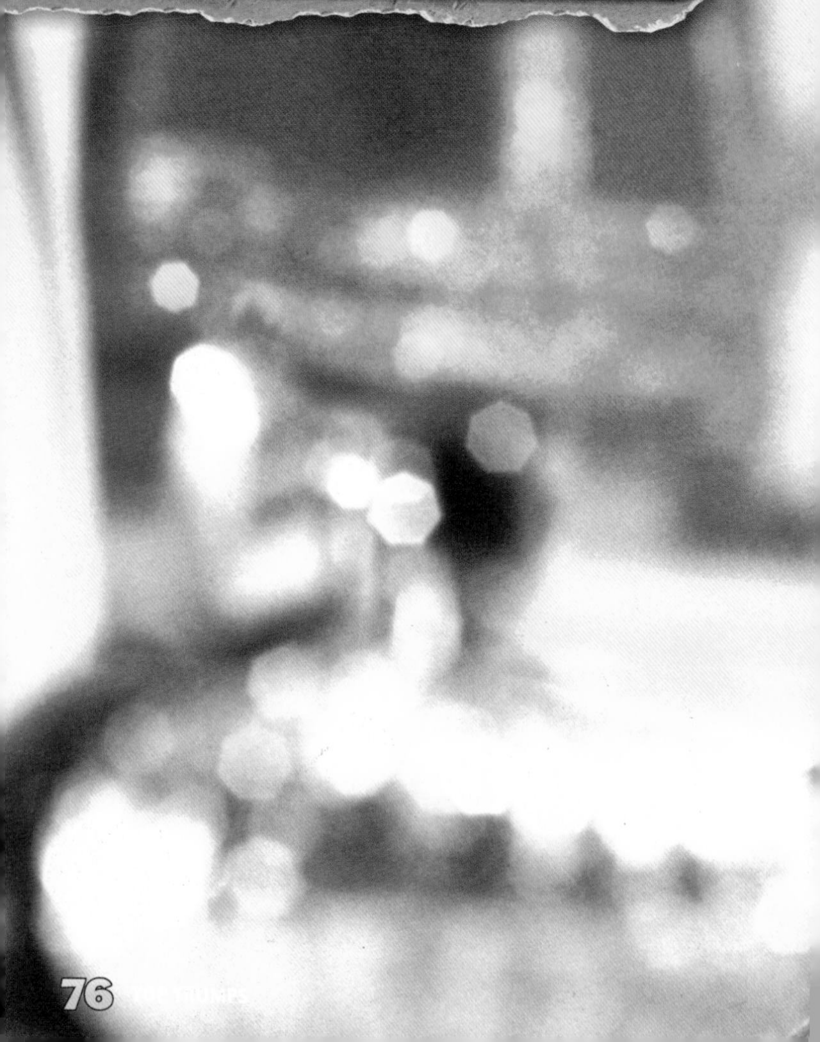

Zalim Singh was Maharajah of the Pankot province in India, making his home in Pankot Palace. The young boy ascended to the position of Maharajah when his father passed away. As Maharajah, Singh had the authority to level justice against those who committed offenses in his realm.

When Indiana Jones asked about the resurgence of the Thuggee cult of Kali Ma, Singh assured the professor that the cult was no more. Little did Singh know that he had fallen prey to the cult, a victim of the Black Sleep, and was under the control of Mola Ram and Chattar Lal, who had trained the young ruler in the deadly art of krtya dolls, one of which the zombie used against Indiana as he fought to escape the bowels of Pankot Palace's hidden temple. Singh awakened from the Black Sleep after Short Round shocked him into consciousness, and he told Short Round how to escape the cavernous abyss.

STATISTICS

APPEARANCE:	*Indiana Jones and the Temple of Doom*
STRENGTH LEVEL:	6
INTELLIGENCE LEVEL:	9
SKILLS:	10 Leadership
EQUIPMENT:	8 Krtya dolls, Pins, Dagger
SECONDARY SKILLS:	8 Thuggee black magic arts
ALLEGIANCE:	Pankot, Kali Ma
ENEMIES:	Indiana Jones, Short Round, Willie Scott
ALLIES:	Mola Ram, Chattar Lal
LINE:	**"I am ashamed of what happened here so many years ago, and I assure you this will never happen again in my kingdom."**

MOLA RAM

Mola Ram was one of the few remaining High Priests of the Thuggee cult of Kali Ma. Ram worked in the shadow realm of the diamond mines beneath Pankot Palace, where he strove to restore the goddess Kali to her former glory through horrifying rituals and brainwashing tactics—and the recovery of all the sacred Sankara stones. With the Maharajah of Pankot Province under his control, the evil Mola Ram kidnapped children of surrounding villages and enslaved them in the mines below the palace, forcing them to dig for the stones. He also kidnapped villagers for human sacrifice.

Indiana Jones discovered Ram's underground cult of death and attempted to retrieve sacred stones that would cease Ram's power, but Ram caught him and forced him into the Black Sleep. Short Round was able to wake Jones from his zombie-like state, and Short Round, Indy and Willie escaped Pankot Palace. Mola Ram followed them, though, and tried to kill Jones on a bridge that connected two cliffs. Ram ultimately failed, and fell to the waiting crocodiles in the river below.

STATISTICS

APPEARANCE:	*Indiana Jones and the Temple of Doom*
STRENGTH LEVEL:	**9**
INTELLIGENCE LEVEL:	**9**
SKILLS:	**9** Cult Leadership
EQUIPMENT:	**9** Chalice, Dagger
SECONDARY SKILLS:	**9** Thuggee black magic arts
ALLEGIANCE:	Kali Ma
ENEMIES:	Indiana Jones, Willie Scott, Short Round, Phillip Blumburtt
ALLIES:	Chattar Lal, Zalim Singh
LINE:	**"Soon we will have all five Sankara stones and the Thuggees will be all powerful."**

CAPTAIN PHILLIP BLUMBURTT

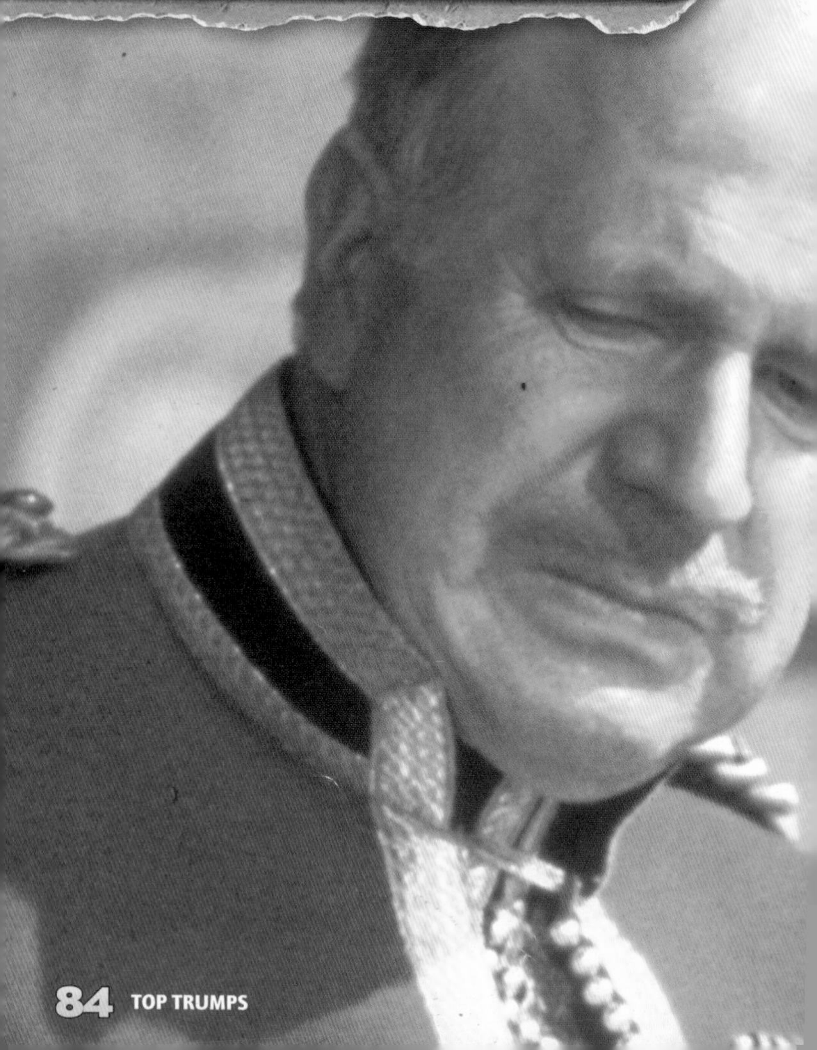

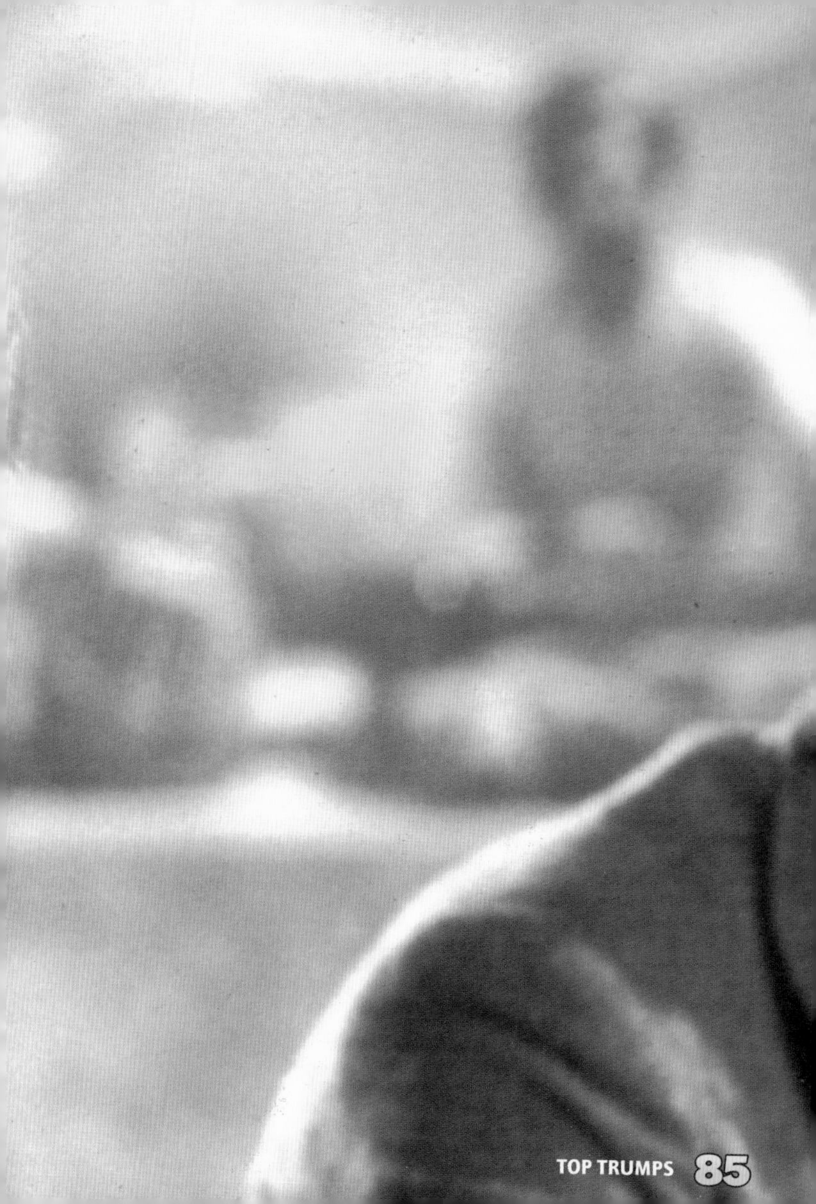

CAPTAIN PHILLIP BLUMBURTT

Captain Phillip James Blumburtt was an officer of the 11th Poona Rifles, a unit of the British military stationed in India during England's waning years of rule in the country. Among Captain Blumburtt's duties was responsibility for patrolling Pankot Province and ensuring its stability. Captain Blumburtt met Indiana Jones during a lavish meal at Pankot Palace hosted by Maharajah Zalim Singh. During the evening, as Jones and the Captain talked, Blumburtt referred to various Thuggee statuary as "mumbo-jumbo," but Jones pointed out that some of the idols had been recently carved.

Blumburtt's dismissal of Thuggee activity as "mumbo-jumbo" turned out to be a cover; he had actually been in Pankot investigating villages' plight, and arrived with his 11th Poona Rifles just in time to save Indiana, Willie and Short Round from Mola Ram's Thuggee warriors as they escaped Pankot Palace.

STATISTICS

APPEARANCE:	*Indiana Jones and the Temple of Doom*
STRENGTH LEVEL:	**7**
INTELLIGENCE LEVEL:	**9**
SKILLS:	**9** Military leadership
EQUIPMENT:	**9** Rifle
SECONDARY SKILLS:	**8** Diplomacy
ALLEGIANCE:	British Government
ENEMIES:	Mola Ram, Chattar Lal
ALLIES:	Indiana Jones, 11th Poona Rifles
LINE:	**"The Thuggee was an obscenity that worshipped Kali with human sacrifices. The British Army nicely did away with them."**

MARHAN

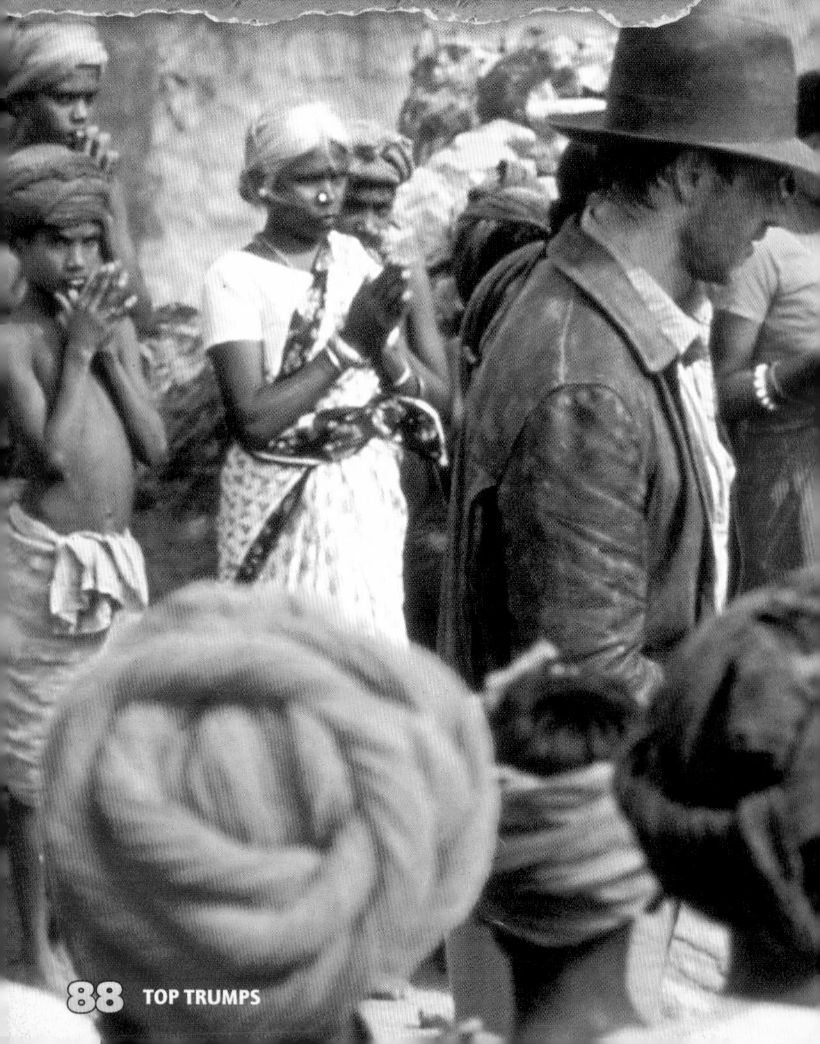

MARHAN

After their escape from certain doom on their flight from Shanghai, Dr. Jones, Willie Scott and Short Round found themselves floating down the Yamuna River in India. On shore, they met the holy man Marhan. When Indiana saw the devastation in Mayapore Village, he asked Marhan what had happened. Marhan explained that the Sankara Stone had been stolen and the village's children kidnapped by the Thuggee at Pankot Palace, which had consequently wreaked destruction and famine on the village. Only if the villagers pledged allegiance to Kali Ma would their children be returned to them.

After giving Indiana, Short Round, and Willie portions of the village's only remaining food, Marhan told Indy that Shiva had sent him to go to Pankot Palace to retrieve the Shiva Linga and restore health to the dying village.

After Indiana Jones had succeeded in his mission to take back Mayapore's missing Sankara Stone, life returned to the village and Marhan knew that Jones would return with the sacred stone and the children.

STATISTICS

APPEARANCE:	*Indiana Jones and the Temple of Doom*
STRENGTH LEVEL:	4
INTELLIGENCE LEVEL:	9
SKILLS:	8 Wisdom
EQUIPMENT:	10 Shiva Linga
SECONDARY SKILLS:	9 Leadership, Persuasion
ALLEGIANCE:	Shiva
ENEMIES:	The Thuggee
ALLIES:	Indiana Jones, Willie Scott, Short Round
LINE:	**"We know you are coming back, when life return to our village. Now, you can see the miracle of the rock."**

HERMAN MUELLER

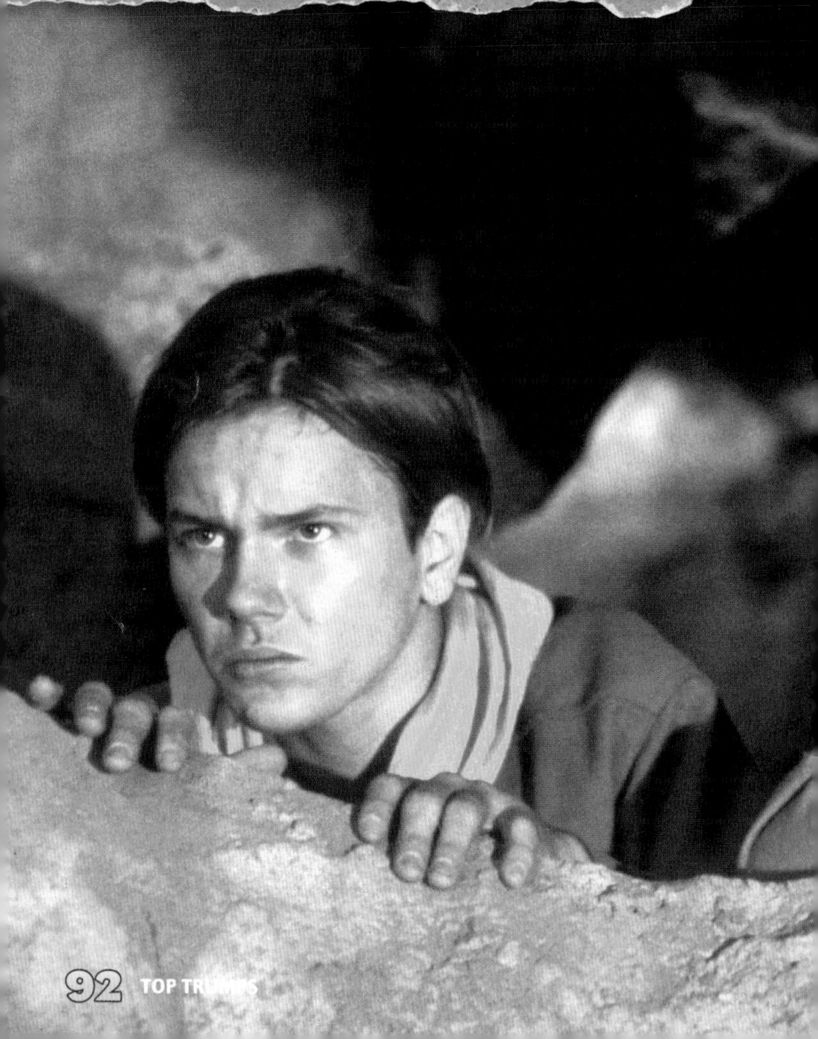

HERMAN MUELLER

Herman Mueller was one of Indiana Jones' scouting companions on an equestrian camping trip in Utah in 1912. When Mueller and Jones discovered "Fedora" and workers looting a treasure site, Jones stayed in the cave in order to retrieve the Cross of Coronado and told Mueller to get the sheriff and report the looters. Mueller raced away as Jones snuck away with the artifact, only to be discovered and chased through harrowing circumstances to his home.

As Indy tried to explain the situation to his father, a bugle sounded in the distance – Mueller had arrived with the sheriff. The law man turned out to be less than Indy had hoped for when he demanded that Indy hand over the Cross of Coronado to "Fedora," an agent for its rightful owner – the man in the Panama hat.

STATISTICS

APPEARANCE:	*Indiana Jones and the Last Crusade*
STRENGTH LEVEL:	**5**
INTELLIGENCE LEVEL:	**6**
SKILLS:	**6** Scouting
EQUIPMENT:	**4** Bugle
SECONDARY SKILLS:	**4** Bugling
ALLEGIANCE:	Boy Scouts
ENEMIES:	"Fedora"
ALLIES:	Indiana Jones
LINE:	**"I brought the sheriff!"**

HENRY JONES, SR.

Dr. Henry Jones, Sr. was a medieval literature professor as well as an expert on the Holy Grail. In 1938 he was hired by Walter Donovan to search for the Grail. Jones travelled to Venice to search for the tomb of a Grail Knight, but was kidnapped before he could discover the tomb's location. Before disappearing, he mailed his Grail diary to his son, Indiana, for safe-keeping.

Donovan then hired Indiana to pick up where his father left off, as well as to find his father. Indiana was falling into a trap to bring the Grail diary to his father's captors – the Nazis and Donovan himself. After rescuing his father, Indiana accompanied him on a race to the Grail that ended when Donovan shot Henry, forcing Indiana to recover the Grail and use its healing powers to save his father. Indiana passed the test and healed his father's wounds. After Henry Jones, Sr. gazed at the Grail, his lifelong passion, he pleaded with Indiana to leave it behind, and father and son left the Grail Temple together.

STATISTICS

APPEARANCE:	*Indiana Jones and the Last Crusade*
STRENGTH LEVEL:	**6**
INTELLIGENCE LEVEL:	**10**
SKILLS:	**10** Grail knowledge
EQUIPMENT:	**7** Umbrella
SECONDARY SKILLS:	**10** Medieval Literature
ALLEGIANCE:	Indiana Jones
ENEMIES:	Walter Donovan, Elsa Schneider, Colonel Vogel
ALLIES:	Indiana Jones, Sallah Mohammed Faisel el-Kahir
LINE:	**"You call this archaeology?"**

WALTER DONOVAN

WALTER DONOVAN

A wealthy art and archaeology enthusiast, Walter Donovan was highly respected for his contributions to the National Museum. His home was filled with rare antiquities he had scoured the globe to find, including a fragment of a tablet he believed would lead to the resting place of the Holy Grail. Obsessed with everlasting life, Donovan had hired Henry Jones, Sr., a Grail expert, to recover the other portion of the tablet and ultimately the Grail itself. After Henry Sr. hid his Grail diary, Donovan hired Indiana to take up where his father left off and to find the diary.

Little did Indiana know he was walking into a trap set by Donovan and his co-conspirators, the Nazis. Donovan had used Hitler's passion for occult objects to his own benefit. Donovan didn't care about Hitler's motives as long as he discovered the Grail. When Indiana passed through the three challenges on his way to the Grail sanctuary, Donovan followed. Greedy and impatient, Donovan was led to choose from a number of imposter Grails and drank from the cup – but he chose poorly, aged instantly and died.

STATISTICS

APPEARANCE:	*Indiana Jones and the Last Crusade*
STRENGTH LEVEL:	**6**
INTELLIGENCE LEVEL:	**8**
SKILLS:	**9** Persuasion
EQUIPMENT:	**10** Nazi soldiers, weapons and tanks, Money
SECONDARY SKILLS:	**9** Obsession
ALLEGIANCE:	Greed
ENEMIES:	Henry Jones, Sr., Marcus Brody, Indiana Jones, Sallah Mohammed Faisel el-Kahir
LINE:	**"Didn't I warn you not to trust anybody, Dr. Jones?"**

ELSA SCHNEIDER

ELSA SCHNEIDER

Dr. Elsa Schneider, hired by Adolf Hitler to find the Holy Grail, worked with Walter Donovan in an attempt to wrest Dr. Henry Jones Sr.'s Grail knowledge and diary from him. After Jones discovered her true motives, she had him taken prisoner, and Donovan sent Indiana Jones to join Schneider. Together, Schneider and Indiana discovered the tomb of the Grail Knight below the city of Venice. When Schneider discovered that Indiana had the Grail diary with him, she manipulated him into the hands of the Nazis, then took it from him.

Schneider and Jones met again in Berlin and in the Grail Temple, where Schneider showed a shred of humanity by tricking Walter Donovan into drinking from a cup that was not the Holy Grail. She remained greedy, however, and ignored the Grail Knight's warning not to pass the seal of the Temple with the Grail. She caused an earthquake and fell into a bottomless pit while trying to reach for the Grail as it dangled out of reach on a precipice.

STATISTICS

APPEARANCE:	*Indiana Jones and the Last Crusade*
STRENGTH LEVEL:	**7**
INTELLIGENCE LEVEL:	**10**
SKILLS:	**9** Archaeology, Espionage
EQUIPMENT:	None
SECONDARY SKILLS:	**10** Charm
ALLEGIANCE:	The Grail
ENEMIES:	Indiana Jones, Henry Jones, Sr., Sallah Mohammed Faisel el-Kahir, Dr. Marcus Brody, rats
ALLIES:	Adolf Hitler, Colonel Vogel, Walter Donovan
LINE:	**"I believe in the Grail, not the swastika."**

KAZIM

Kazim, a descendant of the Princess of the Christian Empire of Byzantium, was a member of the Brotherhood of the Cruciform Sword, sworn to defend the Holy Grail from its enemies. As such, he travelled to Venice, Italy, from Iskenderun when he discovered that Dr. Jones was searching for the Grail. He led a party of the Brotherhood of the Cruciform Sword into a library where Indiana and Elsa had discovered a passage to a Grail Knight's tomb. He set the catacombs ablaze to stop Indy, but failed. He then chased Indy and Elsa through a Venice lagoon on speedboats. When Indy told Kazim he was searching for his father, not the Grail – Kazim told him where his father was being held.

Kazim and the Brotherhood later attacked a Nazi caravan as it searched for the Canyon of the Crescent Moon, the resting place of the Holy Grail, and was mortally wounded in the ensuing battle.

STATISTICS

APPEARANCE:	*Indiana Jones and the Last Crusade*
STRENGTH LEVEL:	**8**
INTELLIGENCE LEVEL:	**7**
SKILLS:	**8** Battle
EQUIPMENT:	**8** Machine gun
SECONDARY SKILLS:	**8** Devotion
ALLEGIANCE:	Brotherhood of the Cruciform Sword
ENEMIES:	Walter Donovan, Elsa Schneider, Colonel Vogel
ALLIES:	Indiana Jones, Brotherhood of the Cruciform Sword
LINE:	**"My soul is prepared."**

COLONEL VOGEL

COLONEL VOGEL

Loyal only to Der Führer, Colonel Ernst Vogel did not care about the Holy Grail in the slightest – only that Hitler attained his prize. He was ruthless and brutal in his tactics as middle-man between Hitler and Dr. Schneider. After Vogel pretended to threaten his compatriot Elsa Schneider's life, Jones surrendered his father's Grail diary, despite his father's protests, only to discover that he had been set up. After the Joneses escaped captivity and travelled to Berlin to retrieve the diary, Vogel found them attempting to escape Germany on a zeppelin. Indiana threw him from the dirigible. The humiliation further fuelled Vogel's need for revenge. He thought he was going to get it when he had Indiana hanging from a tank turret being dragged to his presumed death, but Indiana recovered and fought Vogel atop the tank, which sped out of control over a cliff. Though Indiana was able to leap from the contraption, Vogel was not, and plummeted to his doom.

STATISTICS

APPEARANCE:	*Indiana Jones and the Last Crusade*
STRENGTH LEVEL:	**7**
INTELLIGENCE LEVEL:	**7**
SKILLS:	**7** Hand-to-hand combat, Weaponry
EQUIPMENT:	**6** Pistol
SECONDARY SKILLS:	**7** Military Duty
ALLEGIANCE:	Nazis
ENEMIES:	Henry Jones, Sr., Indiana Jones, Dr. Marcus Brody, Sallah Mohammed Faisel el-Kahir
ALLIES:	Walter Donovan, Elsa Schneider
LINE:	**"This is how we say goodbye in Germany, Dr. Jones."**

MUTT WILLIAMS

Mutt Williams, a rebellious motorcycle-riding youth, came looking for Indiana Jones with a letter from his mother. Jones, according to the letter, was the only person who could find her and their friend Harold Oxley, both of whom were missing in Peru. Williams and Jones travelled to Peru and found a crystal skull in an ancient graveyard, only to be taken prisoner by KGB operative Dr. Irina Spalko, who had also been searching for the skull. They travelled to a KGB camp in the middle of the Amazon, where Williams was reunited with his mother Marion Ravenwood and their friend Harold Oxley. After an escape attempt, Williams was tied up in the back of a KGB truck with Indiana and Marion, who told him that Indiana was his real father. At first he refused to believe it, but got used to the idea after surviving a chase through the Amazon rain forest, a sword fight with Irina Spalko and an attack by giant ants. He then helped his father defeat the KGB and return the crystal skull to its rightful place at Akator.

Williams watched happily as his mother married his father back in a small chapel in the United States.

STATISTICS

APPEARANCE:	*Indiana Jones and the Kingdom of the Crystal Skull*
STRENGTH LEVEL:	8
INTELLIGENCE LEVEL:	7
SKILLS:	8 Swordfighting
EQUIPMENT:	8 Switchblade, Sword, Motorcycle
SECONDARY SKILLS:	9 Motorcycle riding
ALLEGIANCE:	Indiana Jones
ENEMIES:	Irina Spalko, George McHale, Antonin Dovchenko
ALLIES:	Indiana Jones, Harold Oxley, Marion Ravenwood
LINE:	**"You're a teacher?"**

GEORGE McHALE

Mac, as Indy called him, was a former operative in England's secret intelligence service. He and Indiana had been partnered on many missions during World War II and had become very good friends. Mac had saved Indy's life on more than one occasion and Indy thought he could trust Mac completely. After being captured by Russian spies in Mexico, Mac and Indy were taken to a secret military base, Hangar 51, where Jones was expected to help Russians find an alien mummy and ultimately a crystal skull. When Indy tried to escape, Mac revealed that he was actually working for the Russians because they "paid well." Mac, in debt due to gambling, had traded in his values for cash. He helped the Russians throughout their quest for the crystal skull and Akator, even after tricking Jones into believing that he was actually a CIA operative. He left markers for the Russians that led them to Akator. After Jones replaced the crystal skull and a rift in dimensions was opened, Mac, greedy to the end, got sucked into another dimension while trying to grab at treasure.

STATISTICS

APPEARANCE:	*Indiana Jones and the Kingdom of the Crystal Skull*
STRENGTH LEVEL:	**6**
INTELLIGENCE LEVEL:	**6**
SKILLS:	**7** Double-crossing
EQUIPMENT:	**7** Pistol
SECONDARY SKILLS:	None
ALLEGIANCE:	KGB
ENEMIES:	Indiana Jones, Mutt Williams
ALLIES:	Antonin Dovchenko, Irina Spalko
LINE:	**"Just like Berlin."**

IRINA SPALKO

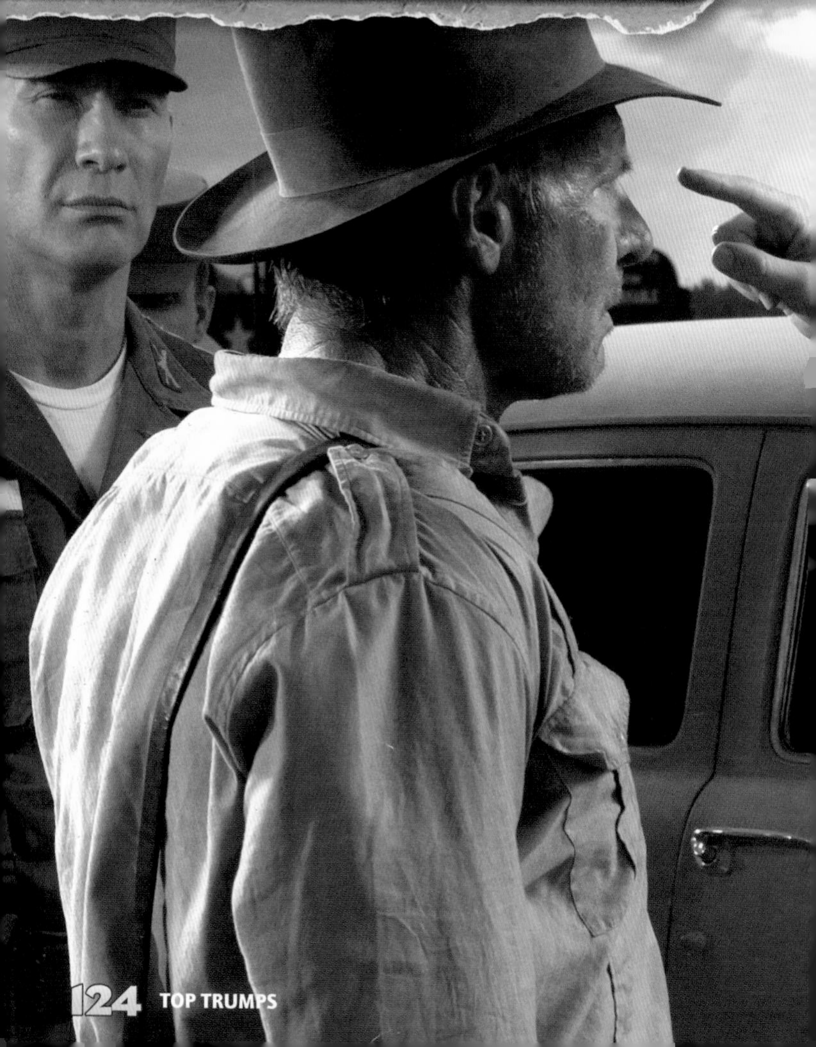

IRINA SPALKO

Legends stated that the person who possessed the crystal skull of Akator would have the power to control the entire world. Dr. Irina Spalko, in charge of researching psychic warfare for the U.S.S.R., was obsessed with finding this skull and using its powers against Russia's enemies.

Her obsession led her to the Amazonian jungle where she and her operatives held Indiana Jones, Mutt Williams, Harold Oxley and Marion Williams captive as they tried to force Jones to unlock the skull's secret. Ultimately, Jones escaped, and Spalko chased him through the jungle to Akator, where, after Jones had returned the crystal skull to its crystal skeleton, Spalko demanded that the skull tell her everything. The knowledge the skull imbued was too much for Spalko's brain to contain, and she perished in a psychic burst.

STATISTICS

APPEARANCE:	*Indiana Jones and the Kingdom of the Crystal Skull*
STRENGTH LEVEL:	**8**
INTELLIGENCE LEVEL:	**10**
SKILLS:	**10** Leadership, Espionage, Swordfighting
EQUIPMENT:	**10** Rapier, Machine Gun
SECONDARY SKILLS:	**10** Multiple Languages, Psychic powers
ALLEGIANCE:	KGB
ENEMIES:	Indiana Jones, Mutt Williams, Marion Williams, Harold Oxley
ALLIES:	Antonin Dovchenko, George McHale
LINE:	**"I want to know!"**

ANTONIN DOVCHENKO

Assigned to work with Irina Spalko, Dovchenko was a member of the KGB special forces that kidnapped Indiana Jones and infiltrated a United States military compound in search of an alien being. Jones escaped in the massive hangar, and Dovchenko pursued him. The two landed on an experimental rocket sled, which was inadvertently activated. As they sped at top speed out of the compound, they got the wind knocked out of them and Jones managed to escape.

Dovchenko met Jones again in Peru where the Russians captured him after he discovered where Harold Oxley had hidden the crystal skull of Akator. Against his will, Jones deciphered Akator's location. After Jones managed to escape his binds and commandeer a truck from the Russians, a chase ensued through the Amazonian jungle. After careening into a huge mound, Jones and Dovchenko engaged in hand-to-hand combat, but Dovchenko lost when a mound of flesh-eating ants attacked and devoured him.

STATISTICS

APPEARANCE:	*Indiana Jones and the Kingdom of the Crystal Skull*
STRENGTH LEVEL:	**10**
INTELLIGENCE LEVEL:	**6**
SKILLS:	**9** Hand-to-hand combat
EQUIPMENT:	**9** Machine gun
SECONDARY SKILLS:	**8** Loyalty, Gun
ALLEGIANCE:	KGB
ENEMIES:	Indiana Jones, Marion Williams, Mutt Williams, Harold Oxley
ALLIES:	Irina Spalko

HAROLD OXLEY

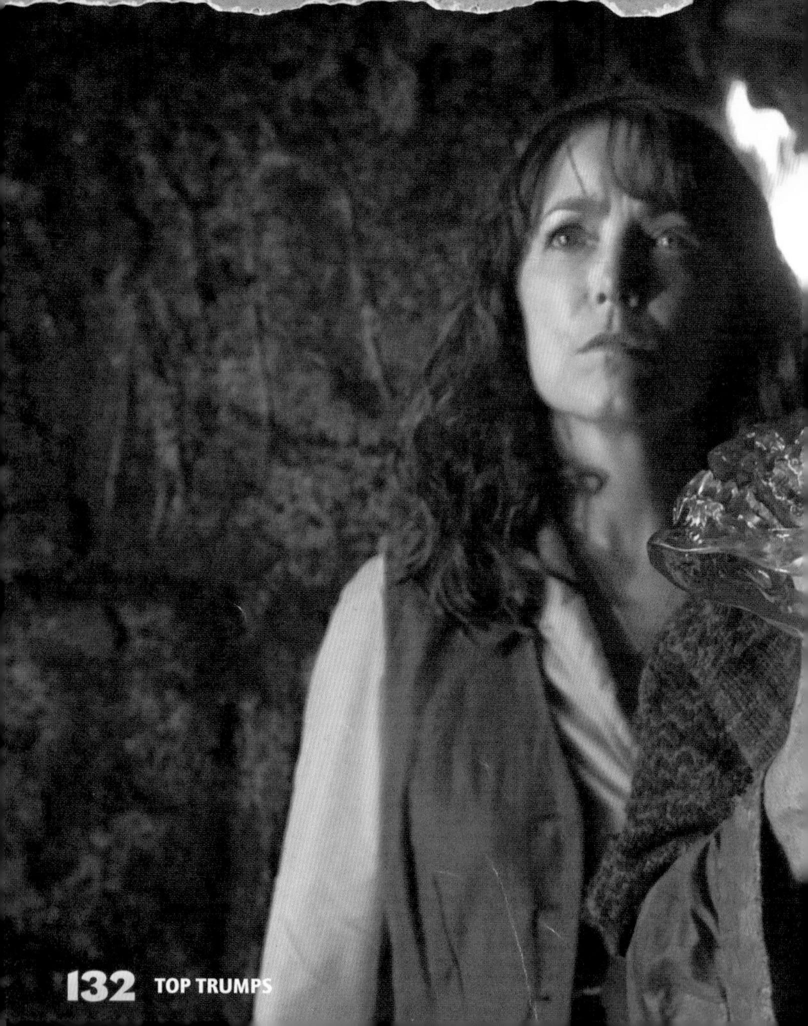

HAROLD OXLEY

Indiana Jones was surprised when Mutt Williams approached him, telling him that his estranged friend Harold Oxley had gone missing while searching for the crystal skull of Akator.

Oxley had been obsessed with the legend of the skull, and had managed to find the mystical artifact and Akator. He couldn't solve the riddle of entry to the lost city, so he returned the skull to its hiding place – but had gazed into its eyes too long and gone mad. He had therefore been imprisoned in an asylum, where he drew a map to the skull's location. Indiana, on a quest to find Oxley, found the map he had drawn, and recovered the skull. When Indiana was reunited with Oxley, who had been kidnapped by Irina Spalko, he was able to decipher the gibberish Oxley was speaking, and together the two found the entrance to the lost city. After the skull was back with its rightful owner, Oxley's sanity came back to him.

STATISTICS

APPEARANCE:	*Indiana Jones and the Kingdom of the Crystal Skull*
STRENGTH LEVEL:	5
INTELLIGENCE LEVEL:	10
SKILLS:	**10** Psychic connection with the crystal skull
EQUIPMENT:	**10** Crystal skull
SECONDARY SKILLS:	**10** Knowledge of Akator's location
ALLEGIANCE:	Indiana Jones
ENEMIES:	Irina Spalko
ALLIES:	Marion Williams, Mutt Williams, Indiana Jones
LINE:	**"Three times it drops."**

DEAN CHARLES STANFORTH

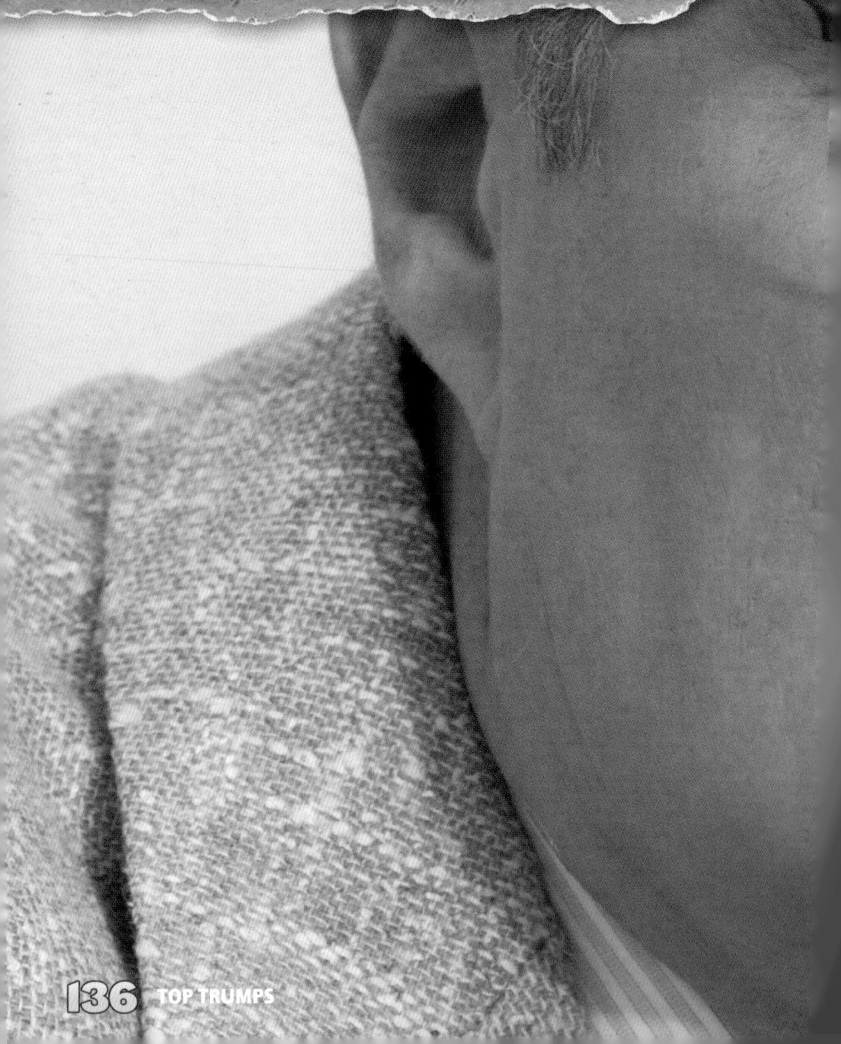

DEAN CHARLES STANFORTH

Stanforth had the bittersweet privilege of replacing Charles Brody as Dean of Students at Marshall College after Brody had passed away. He also had the unpleasant duty to inform Indiana Jones that the professor was being placed on a leave of absence after his entanglements with the KGB had made U.S. intelligence suspicious of his allegiances. As an act of protest and in order to keep Jones from being fired, Stanforth resigned his position as dean of the college. After Jones was cleared of all charges, Stanforth was reinstated at the College and watched happily as Jones, who had recently been promoted to Associate Dean of the college, and his long-lost love, Marion Williams, were married.

STATISTICS

APPEARANCE:	*Indiana Jones and the Kingdom of the Crystal Skull*
STRENGTH LEVEL:	**6**
INTELLIGENCE LEVEL:	**8**
SKILLS:	**8** Leadership
EQUIPMENT:	None
SECONDARY SKILLS:	**8** Loyalty
ALLEGIANCE:	Indiana Jones
ENEMIES:	None
ALLIES:	Indiana Jones
LINE:	**"I resigned."**

INTERDIMENSIONAL BEINGS

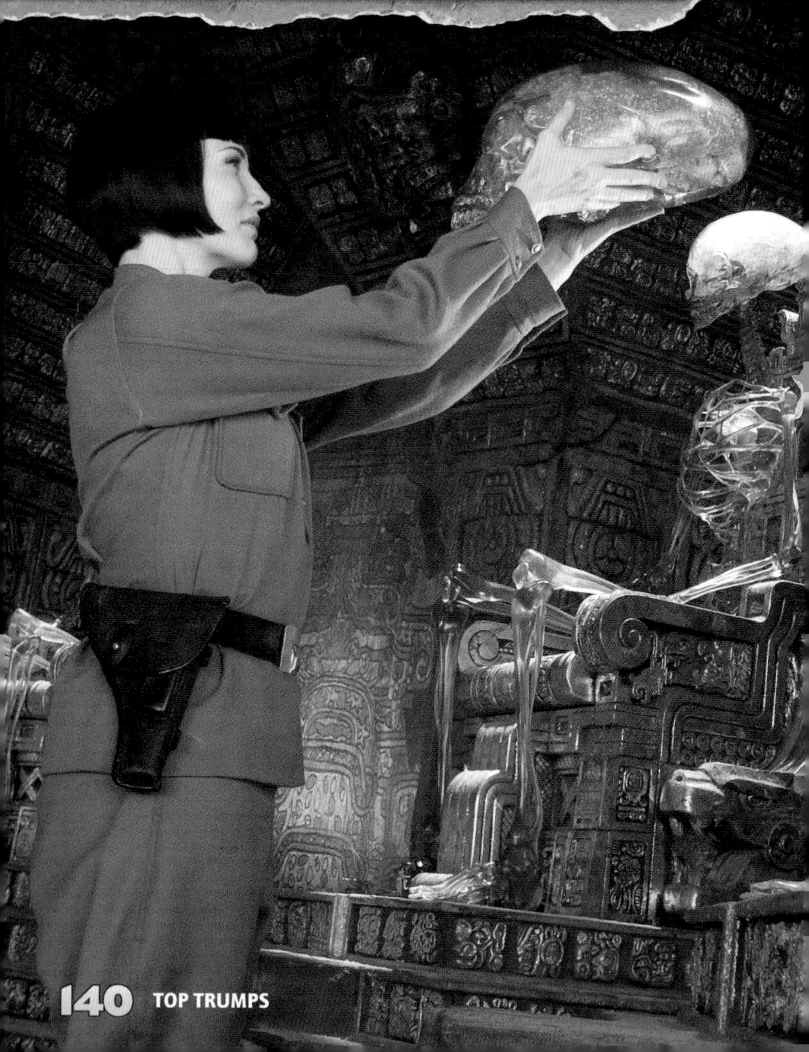

INTERDIMENSIONAL BEINGS

Revered by ancient South Americans as gods, these aliens from another dimension were, according to Indiana Jones, archaeologists who had come to Earth to study it, bestowing upon the early people of Akator basic laws and early technology. When one of the beings' skulls was stolen by the Spanish Conquistador Orellana, Akator was lost to the jungle, but legends of the crystal skull persisted – he who returned the skull to Akator, the city of gold, would have an incredible gift.

Indiana Jones, in a fight against time and Dr. Irina Spalko, managed to return the alien's skull to the inner chamber. Spalko, however, took the skull from Indy and gave it to the creature. In gratitude, the being wanted to give her a gift. Spalko demanded to know "everything." But she couldn't contain its vast intelligence and died. Afterward, the being opened an interdimensional rift. As Indiana, Oxley, Mutt and Marion watched, an enormous, saucerlike craft revealed itself and entered the rift. Afterward, the land where Akator had once stood flooded and became an enormous lake.

STATISTICS

APPEARANCE:	*Indiana Jones and the Kingdom of the Crystal Skull*
STRENGTH LEVEL:	**10**
INTELLIGENCE LEVEL:	**10**
SKILLS:	**10** Omniscience
EQUIPMENT:	**10** Flying Saucer
SECONDARY SKILLS:	**10** Interdimensional Travel
ALLEGIANCE:	Its hivelike compatriots
ENEMIES:	None
ALLIES:	Indiana Jones, Harold Oxley

GRAIL KNIGHT

GRAIL KNIGHT

The last of three brothers who had sworn a sacred oath to protect the Holy Grail from its enemies, the Grail Knight had stood watch over it in a well-protected sanctuary in the Grail Temple for over 700 years. When Indiana Jones managed to pass the three challenges and enter the Grail room, the Knight mistakenly thought Indiana had come to steal the cup and attempted to do battle. Too old, the knight raised his sword but fell backward. He then attempted to pass the responsibility of protecting the Grail on to Indiana, but before he could, Walter Donovan and Elsa Schneider entered the room. The Knight instructed Donovan to choose wisely when picking a cup from which to drink. After Donovan failed, Indiana chose the actual Grail, but was warned that the cup could not pass the Great Seal on the floor of the Temple. After Elsa ignored the knight's admonitions and the Temple turned to rubble, Indiana and Henry Jones, Sr. turned to see the Grail Knight bidding them farewell.

STATISTICS

APPEARANCE:	*Indiana Jones and the Last Crusade*
STRENGTH LEVEL:	**3**
INTELLIGENCE LEVEL:	**9**
SKILLS:	**10** Devotion
EQUIPMENT:	**6** Sword
SECONDARY SKILLS:	**10** Everlasting life
ALLEGIANCE:	The Holy Grail
ENEMIES:	Walter Donovan, Elsa Schneider
ALLIES:	God, Henry Jones, Sr.
LINE:	**"He chose poorly."**

NAZIS

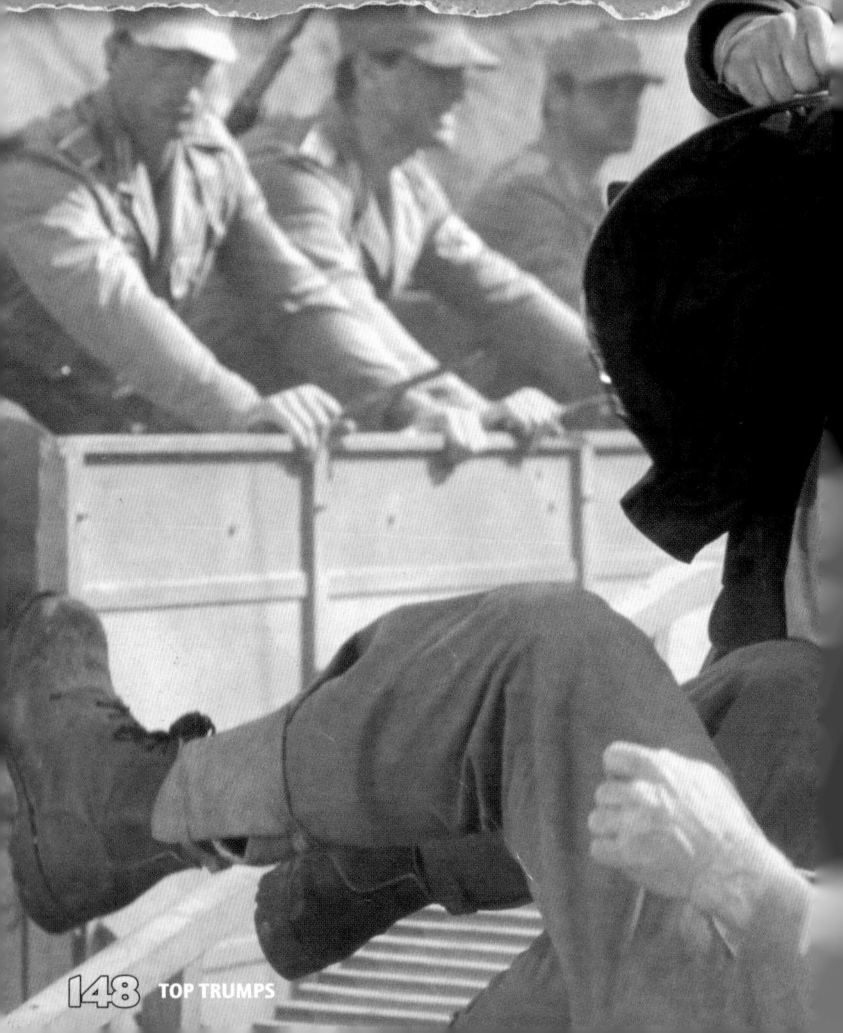

NAZIS

The National Socialist Party, or Nazis for short, gained control over Germany in 1933. Their reign spread over much of Europe after they started World War II by invading Poland. Unthinking in their devotion to their leader, Adolf Hitler, these soldiers were merciless and stopped at nothing to gain glory for their homeland. When Hitler expressed interest in occult items, Nazi parties were sent all over the globe in attempts to retrieve them.

Indiana Jones ran into Nazis on several occasions, most notably in his quest for the lost Ark of the Covenant and the Holy Grail, both artifacts of unmentionable power that, if in the wrong hands, could have wreaked destruction on the Earth. Jones managed to outsmart the Nazis, however, and the artifacts remained safe.

STATISTICS

APPEARANCE:	*Indiana Jones and the Raiders of the Lost Ark, Indiana Jones and the Last Crusade*
STRENGTH LEVEL:	**8**
INTELLIGENCE LEVEL:	**6**
SKILLS:	**9** Battle, Hand-to-hand Combat
EQUIPMENT:	**10** Machine guns, Pistols, Tanks, Planes, Submarines
SECONDARY SKILLS:	**8** Unflinching devotion
ALLEGIANCE:	Adolf Hitler
ENEMIES:	The World
ALLIES:	Italy, Japan

THUGGEE

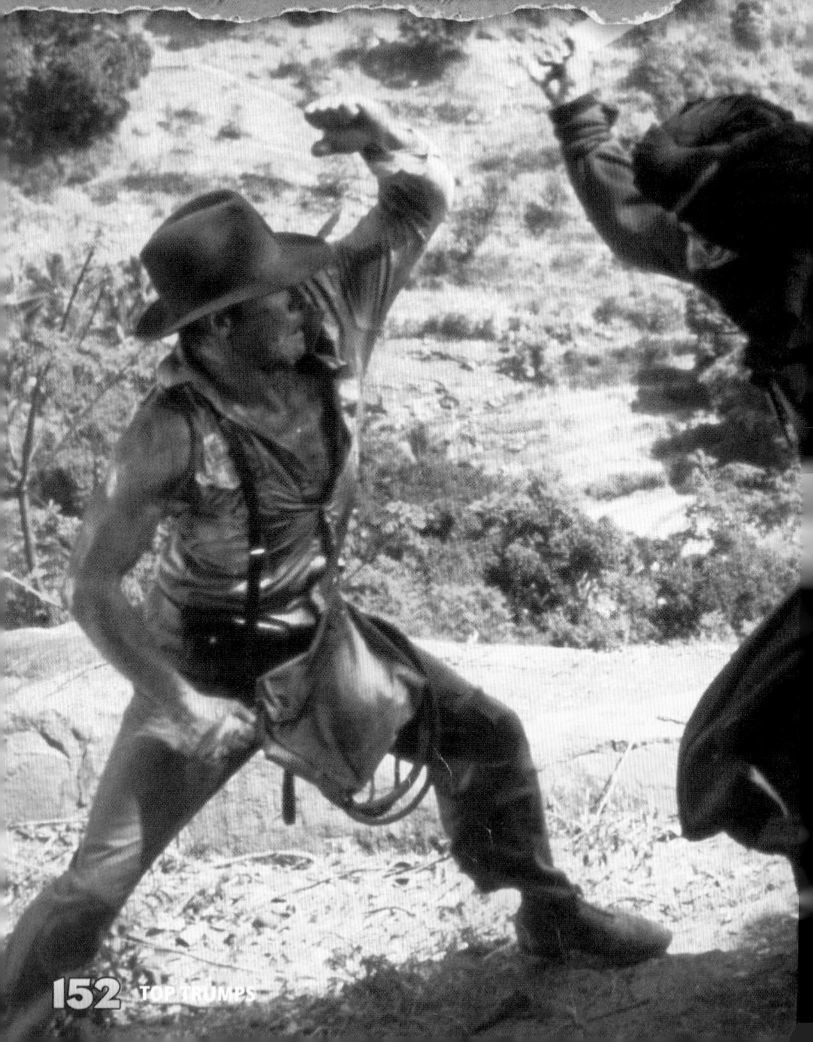

THUGGEE

An ancient blood and death cult that worshipped the goddess Kali, the Thuggee had at one point overrun the area surrounding Pankot Palace, kidnapping unwitting travellers and villagers in order to sacrifice them in their bloody rituals. British troops, alerted to the Thuggee terror cult's presence, eradicated the fiendish group in the 1800s, or so they thought. The cult persevered, but in secret, operating in the depths below Pankot Palace.

By the time Indiana Jones made his appearance at Pankot Palace, the Thuggee were preparing to make their presence known again. Mola Ram, the High Priest of the cult, had amassed three of five Sankara stones, sacred objects needed to gain ultimate power, but was thwarted in his goal to revive the cult to its former status. The cult presumably died along with Ram and his henchmen, restoring Pankot Palace and the surrounding villages to peace.

STATISTICS

APPEARANCE:	*Indiana Jones and the Temple of Doom*
STRENGTH LEVEL:	**7**
INTELLIGENCE LEVEL:	**6**
SKILLS:	**7** Thuggee Black Magic, Combat
EQUIPMENT:	**8** Scimitars, Daggers, Bows and Arrows
SECONDARY SKILLS:	**6** Blind devotion
ALLEGIANCE:	Kali Ma, Mola Ram
ENEMIES:	Indiana Jones, Phillip Blumburtt, Short Round
ALLIES:	Mola Ram, Zalim Singh, Chattar Lal

HOVITOS

Deep in the Peruvian jungle lived a feared tribe called the Hovitos. These descendants of the Chachapoyan warriors defended their ancestors' temple ferociously and killed anyone who attempted to locate it and plunder its legendary treasures.

As Indiana Jones and his party scoured the jungle for the temple, they came across a sign that the Hovitos were near – Satipo discovered recently fired blowdarts dipped in poison.

After Dr. Jones escaped the temple with the golden idol for which he'd been searching, he found himself faced down by Hovitos warriors, spears raised, and his archrival, Dr. René Belloq. Belloq, who spoke the Hovitos' language, ordered them to attack Dr. Jones after taking the idol from him. The Hovitos chased Dr. Jones through the jungle with spears and blowdarts until he managed to escape in a plane that had been waiting for him on the river.

STATISTICS

APPEARANCE:	*Indiana Jones and the Raiders of the Lost Ark*
STRENGTH LEVEL:	**8**
INTELLIGENCE LEVEL:	**6**
SKILLS:	**8** Battle
EQUIPMENT:	**7** Bows and arrows, Blowdarts
SECONDARY SKILLS:	**10** Jungle survival
ALLEGIANCE:	The golden idol
ENEMIES:	Dr. Indiana Jones, Barranca
ALLIES:	Dr. René Belloq

BROTHERHOOD OF THE CRUCIFORM SWORD

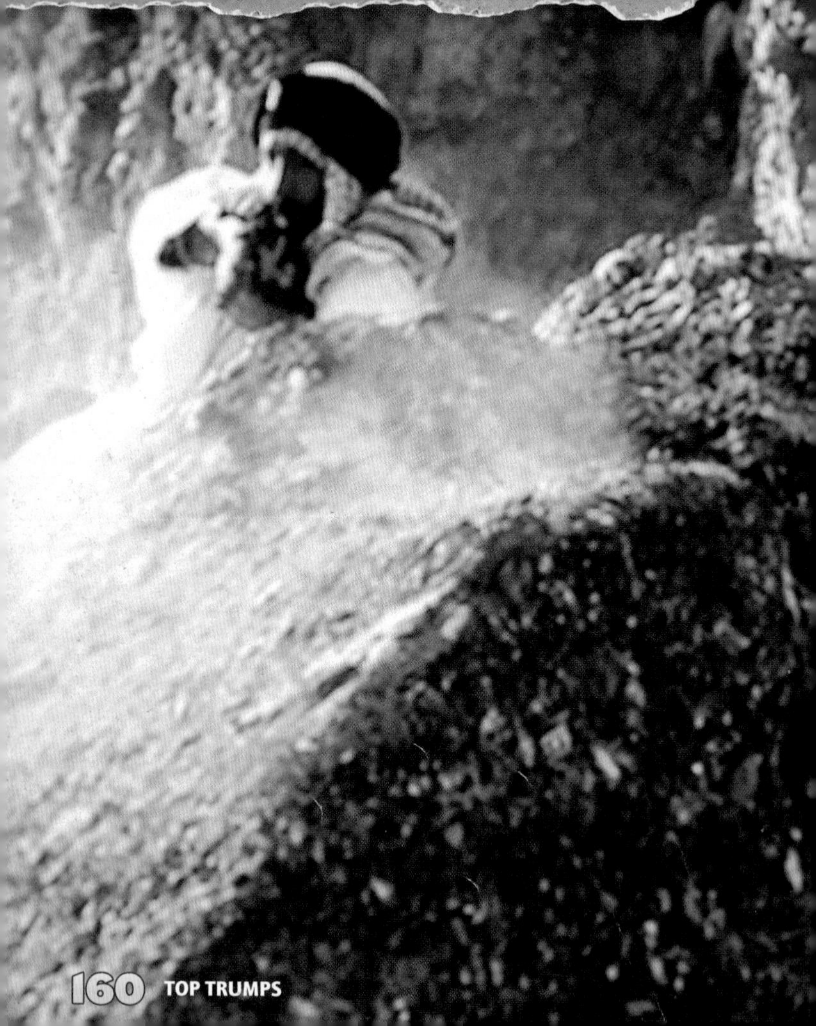

This ancient society was a Brotherhood of people loyal to the Holy Grail and dedicated to protecting it from discovery and misuse. Members of the society often distinguished themselves by having the Cruciform Sword tattooed on their chest.

Members of the brotherhood attempted to stop Indiana Jones from discovering the Grail's location. When in Venice, Jones found clues in a library that led to his discovery a secret passageway. This passage led to a Grail Knight's tomb, and to the Grail's secret location. The Brotherhood knocked out Marcus Brody, who was standing watch, and then set fire to the passageway. Jones and Dr. Schneider managed to escape with the information they needed, but the secret society pursued them. After Jones assured a member that he was not after the Grail, they ended their pursuit. The Brotherhood launched a secret attack against a Nazi caravan that was en route to the Grail's hidden location, but, sadly, lost in the melee.

STATISTICS

APPEARANCE:	*Indiana Jones and the Last Crusade*
STRENGTH LEVEL:	9
INTELLIGENCE LEVEL:	7
SKILLS:	7 Weaponry
EQUIPMENT:	7 Rifles
SECONDARY SKILLS:	8 Devotion
ALLEGIANCE:	The Holy Grail
ENEMIES:	Grail Seekers
ALLIES:	God

UGHA WARRIORS

UGHA WARRIORS

The Ugha people, with the help of their gods, built the majestic city of Akator deep in the Amazon rain forest. Akator, millennia ahead of its time, is thought to be the source from which all other cities came. Its influence on other cultures' architecture, art and culture can be seen throughout South America.

Ugha warriors, descendants of the original builders of Akator, defended the city throughout the centuries. When Indiana Jones and his party arrived at Akator, they discovered a tribe of Ugha Warriors that sprang, it seemed, out of nowhere, having hidden themselves masterfully in the crevices leading to the city. The warriors, experts at using the bola, captured Jones and his party, but backed away when Harold Oxley revealed the crystal skull to them.

STATISTICS

APPEARANCE:	*Indiana Jones and the Kingdom of the Crystal Skull*
STRENGTH LEVEL:	9
INTELLIGENCE LEVEL:	6
SKILLS:	10 Bola
EQUIPMENT:	10 Bola, Spears
SECONDARY SKILLS:	10 Camouflage, Attack
ALLEGIANCE:	Akator
ENEMIES:	Everyone
ALLIES:	The Interdimensional Being

MAJOR EATON

Major Eaton was one of two United States government officials who approached Dr. Jones after the United States intercepted a Nazi communiqué that stated, "Tanis development proceeding. Acquire headpiece, Staff of Ra, Abner Ravenwood, U.S."

Eaton explained to Jones that Hitler had archeologists scouring the globe looking for religious artifacts and that there was a major dig going on outside of Cairo, Egypt. After Jones explained the significance of Tanis – an ancient city that was a possible resting place for the Ark of the Covenant – to Major Eaton and his associate, they commissioned him to go after the Ark and retrieve it before the Nazis could get their hands on it.

After Jones returned with the Ark, Major Eaton refused to tell him what the United States government had done with it, assuring Jones it was in good hands. Major Eaton's refusal to tell Indiana where the Ark was left him frustrated and angry.

STATISTICS

APPEARANCE:	*Indiana Jones and the Raiders of the Lost Ark*
STRENGTH LEVEL:	5
INTELLIGENCE LEVEL:	8
SKILLS:	9 Bureaucracy
EQUIPMENT:	3 Pipe
SECONDARY SKILLS:	8 Evasive talk
ALLEGIANCE:	United States Government
ENEMIES:	Nazi Germany
ALLIES:	Agent Musgrove
LINE:	**"Top men."**

CHEN

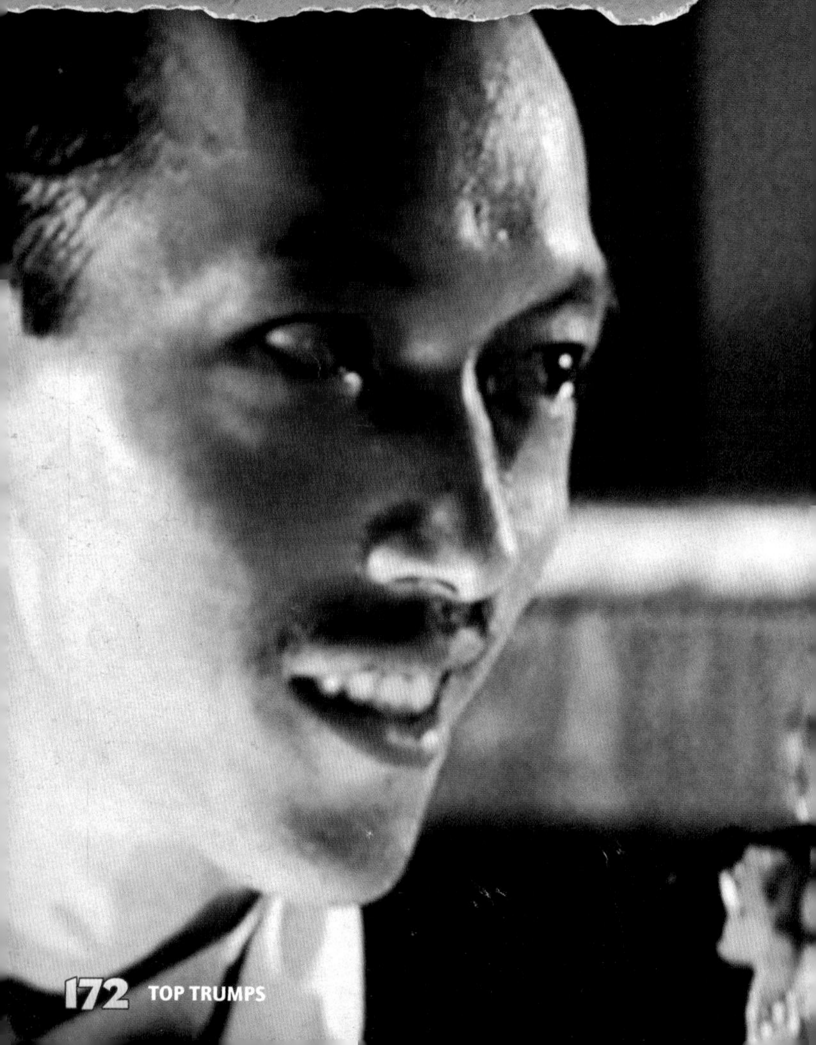

CHEN

Chen was Kao Kan's brother and Lao Che's oldest son. His sinister, wan face revealed his cold and calculating personality. Unlike Kao Kan, Chen said very little and was not subject to acting on impulse.

When Indiana Jones was bargaining with Lao Che for the Eye of the Peacock diamond and it seemed as if Lao Che were going to double-cross him, Indy's friend Wu Han, disguised as a waiter, aimed a pistol at Lao Che in an attempt to get the crime lord to fulfill his end of the bargain. However, as champagne corks popped throughout Club Obi Wan, Chen shot Wu Han without anyone even noticing. Indy avenged his friend when he hurled a flaming skewer at Chen, killing him instantly.

STATISTICS

APPEARANCE:	*Indiana Jones and the Temple of Doom*
STRENGTH LEVEL:	6
INTELLIGENCE LEVEL:	7
SKILLS:	7 Gunfire
EQUIPMENT:	8 Pistol
SECONDARY SKILLS:	7 Crime
ALLEGIANCE:	Lao Che
ENEMIES:	Indiana Jones, Wu Han
ALLIES:	Lao Che, Kao Kan

JOCK LINDSEY

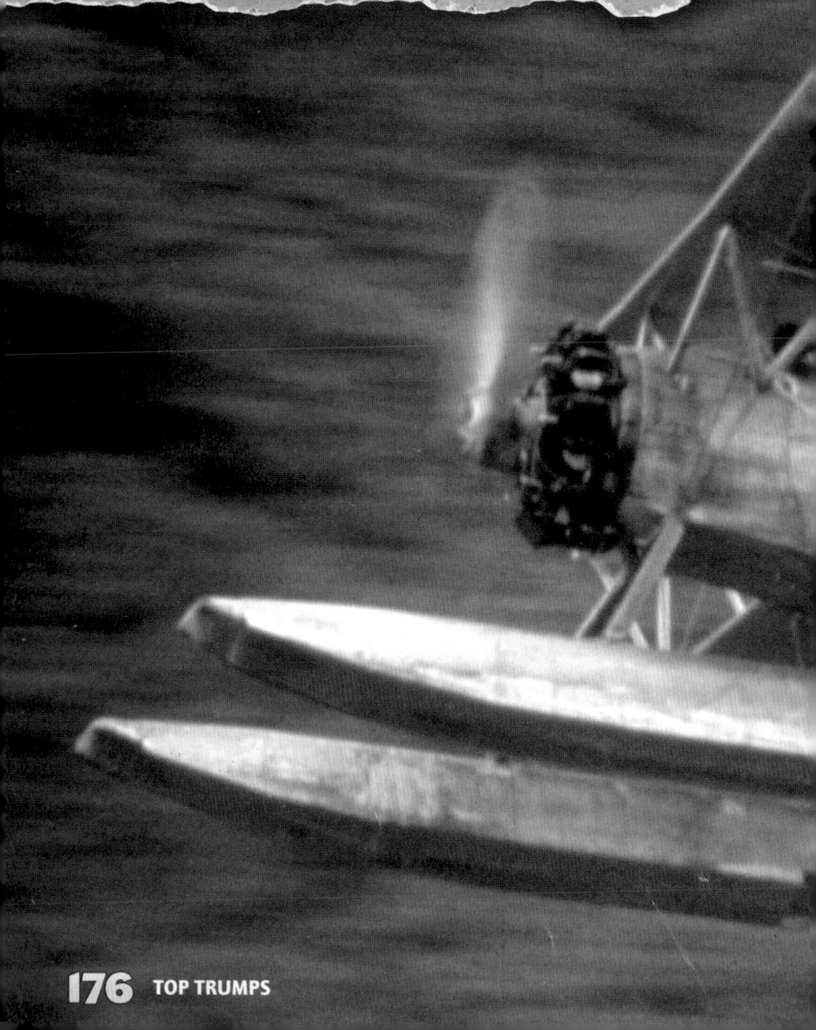

JOCK LINDSEY

Lindsey, a former stunt pilot, flew Indiana Jones deep into the South American jungle on his quest to find an ancient Chachapoyan Temple. Lindsey had planned on spending a few lazy days fishing in a lake tributary where he had landed his amphibious plane.

Lindsey's leisurely day was cut short, however, when Dr. Jones appeared over the horizon being chased by angry Hovitos warriors who, under Dr. René Belloq's instruction, were trying to kill Jones for desecrating their ancestral temple. As Jones approached, Jock realized the dire situation, dropped his fishing pole, and started the engine on his plane.

Jones, who managed to evade blowdarts and arrows as he swam toward the already moving plane, was grateful that Jock had managed the escape, but was less than pleased to meet Jock's pet snake, Reggie.

STATISTICS

APPEARANCE:	*Indiana Jones and the Raiders of the Lost Ark*
STRENGTH LEVEL:	**6**
INTELLIGENCE LEVEL:	**7**
SKILLS:	**10** Piloting
EQUIPMENT:	**10** Amphibious plane
SECONDARY SKILLS:	**7** Fishing
ALLEGIANCE:	Indiana Jones
ENEMIES:	None
ALLIES:	Indiana Jones, Reggie
LINE:	**"That's just my pet snake, Reggie!"**

FEDORA

"Fedora," as he was known due to his fedora hat, led a group of hired treasure hunters on a search in a cave complex in Utah in 1912. Young Indy watched as Fedora found the Cross of Coronado, vowing to seize the treasure and give it to a museum where he felt it belonged. When Fedora's back was turned, Indy stole the cross and escaped with it on horseback. Fedora and his men pursued Indy, who wound up running from them atop the cars of a circus train. Indy escaped his pursuers and ran home with the treasure.

As Indy tried to tell his father what had happened, Fedora and the local sheriff showed up at his house and reclaimed the treasure from him. Although annoyed, Fedora admired Indy's tenacity, and, as a consolation, gave Indy his hat.

STATISTICS

APPEARANCE:	*Indiana Jones and the Last Crusade*
STRENGTH LEVEL:	**9**
INTELLIGENCE LEVEL:	**8**
SKILLS:	**9** Treasure hunting
EQUIPMENT:	**8**
SECONDARY SKILLS:	**9** Horse riding
ALLEGIANCE:	Money
ENEMIES:	Indiana Jones
ALLIES:	Hired hands
LINE:	**"You lost today, kid, but that doesn't mean you have to like it."**

KAO KAN

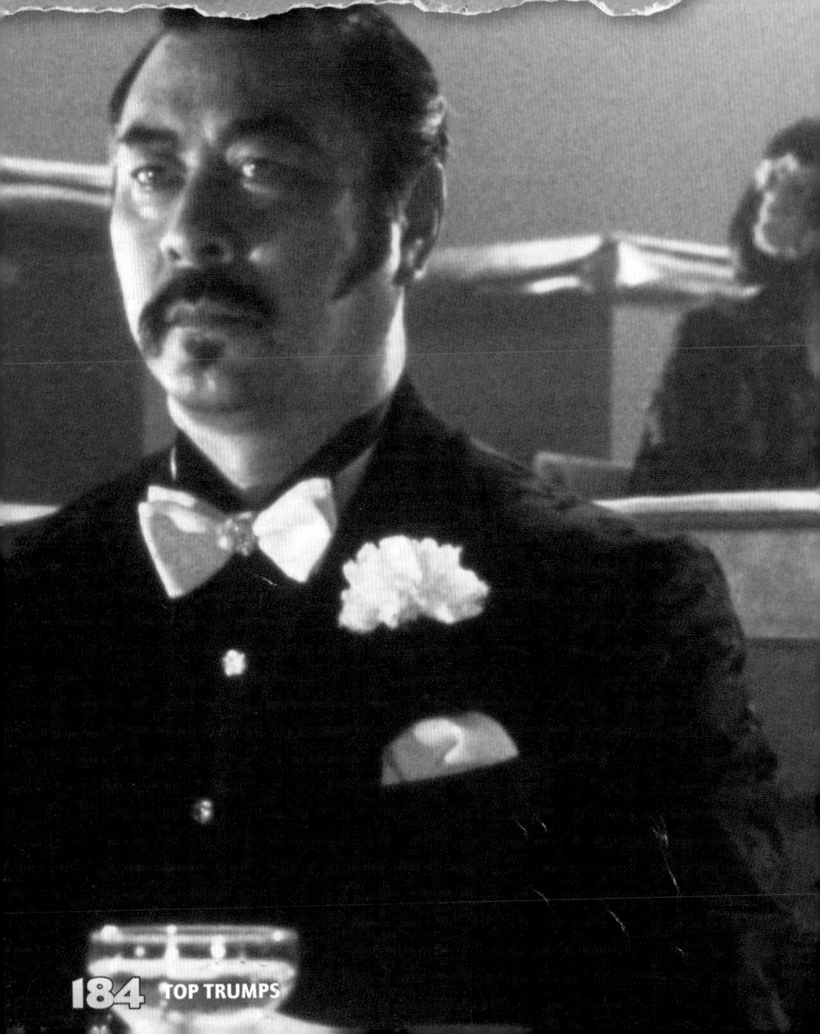

KAO KAN

Kao Kan was crime lord Lao Che's youngest son. Kao Kan had a reputation for rash behavior and a lack of self-control that had, in the past, led Lao Che to use his connections to cover up what were referred to as "youthful indiscretions." Lao Che viewed Kao Kan as the successor to his crime empire in Shanghai.

The night before Indiana Jones was to deliver to Lao Che the urn containing Nurhachi's ashes, Kao Kan attempted to get the treasure without paying. Jones would not give up the urn, and Kao Kan ended up losing a finger in the exchange. The next evening at Club Obi Wan, Kao Kan tried to kill Jones with a submachine gun, but Jones escaped the club. Kao Kan chased Jones to Nang Tao airport, only to watch him escape – in a booby trapped airplane.

STATISTICS

APPEARANCE:	*Indiana Jones and the Temple of Doom*
STRENGTH LEVEL:	**9**
INTELLIGENCE LEVEL:	**6**
SKILLS:	**8** Combat
EQUIPMENT:	**7** Submachine gun
SECONDARY SKILLS:	**7** Crime boss
ALLEGIANCE:	Lao Che
ENEMIES:	Indiana Jones, Willie Scott
ALLIES:	Lao Che, Kao Kan